W9-CPF-925

BRUCE TEGNER presents modern sport judo for recreation, fitness, and health, and as a serious activity for the dedicated athlete.

THROWS & MATWORK GRAPPLING most commonly seen in judo contest today, from intramural play to the Olympic Games, are included, as well as safety falls, strategy and tactics of contest, and a selection of formal routines from traditional judo.

COLORED BELT RANKING guides are given, from beginner through black belt. Step-by-step instruction is clearly explained; photos fully illustrate the techniques.

HUMANISTIC CONCEPTS of physical education are integrated into the approach and the procedures. Safety in practice is emphasized; the text is appropriate for young adults.

STUDENTS & TEACHERS will find this a useful study guide, teaching aid, and reference work.

BOOKS BY BRUCE TEGNER

BRUCE TEGNER'S COMPLETE BOOK of SELF-DEFENSE

BRUCE TEGNER'S COMPLETE BOOK of JUJITSU

SELF-DEFENSE: A BASIC COURSE

SELF-DEFENSE NERVE CENTERS & PRESSURE POINTS

KARATE & JUDO EXERCISES

STICK-FIGHTING: SPORT FORMS

STICK-FIGHTING: SELF-DEFENSE

SAVATE: French Foot & Fist Fighting

AIKIDO & BOKATA

DEFENSE TACTICS for LAW ENFORCEMENT:
  Weaponless Defense & Control and Baton Techniques

KUNG FU & TAI CHI: Chinese Karate & Classical Exercise

KARATE: BEGINNER TO BLACK BELT

JUDO: BEGINNER TO BLACK BELT

BOOKS BY BRUCE TEGNER & ALICE McGRATH

SELF-DEFENSE & ASSAULT PREVENTION FOR GIRLS & WOMEN

SELF-DEFENSE FOR YOUR CHILD

SOLO FORMS OF KARATE, TAI CHI, AIKIDO & KUNG FU

Also available from Thor Publishing Company

ELLEN KEI HUA BOOKS

KUNG FU MEDITATIONS & Chinese Classical Wisdom

WISDOM from the EAST

MEDITATIONS of the MASTERS

JUDO

BEGINNER TO BLACK BELT

BRUCE TEGNER

THOR PUBLISHING COMPANY   VENTURA   CA   93002

Library of Congress Cataloging in Publication Data

Tegner, Bruce
    Judo: Beginner to black belt.
      "Revised version of Bruce Tegner's Complete book of judo"
      -- T. p. verso.
      Includes index.
      1. Judo.   I. Title.
GV1114.T43   1982   796.8'152   82-3192
ISBN 0-87407-521-1   AACR2
ISBN 0-87407-041-4 (pbk.)

*This is a second revised edition of a book originally published
in 1967 under the title Bruce Tegner's Complete Book of Judo.
In this version all text is rewritten and reset; the material is all
reorganized.*

BRUCE TEGNER'S COMPLETE BOOK of JUDO
First edition, July 1967
Second printing, May 1970
Third printing, January 1972
Revised edition, November 1975
Second printing, January 1977
JUDO: BEGINNER to BLACK BELT
First printing, May 1982
Second printing, July 1983

JUDO: BEGINNER to BLACK BELT.
Manuscript prepared under the
supervision of ALICE McGRATH

Copyright © 1967, 1975, 1982 by Bruce Tegner & Alice McGrath

THOR PUBLISHING COMPANY
VENTURA CA 93002

PRINTED IN THE UNITED STATES OF AMERICA

BRUCE TEGNER BOOKS REVIEWED

KARATE: BEGINNER to BLACK BELT
"Techniques and routines...illustrated in profuse detail...
specially geared to a Y.A. audience."
KLIATT YOUNG ADULT PB GUIDE

SELF-DEFENSE: A BASIC COURSE
"An eminently practical, concise guide to self-defense...for
young men..."　American Library Association BOOKLIST

"YA - A calm, nonsexist approach to simple yet effective self-
defense techniques...clear photographs...sound advice."
SCHOOL LIBRARY JOURNAL

BRUCE TEGNER'S COMPLETE BOOK OF JUJITSU
"...authoritative and easy-to-follow text..."
SCHOOL LIBRARY JOURNAL

BRUCE TEGNER'S COMPLETE BOOK OF SELF-DEFENSE
Recommended for Y.A. in the American Library Association
BOOKLIST

SELF-DEFENSE & ASSAULT PREVENTION FOR GIRLS & WOMEN (with
Alice McGrath)
"...should be required reading for all girls and women..."
WILSON LIBRARY BULLETIN

"...simple and straightforward with no condescension...easy to
learn and viable as defense tactics..."　SCHOOL LIBRARY JOURNAL

SELF-DEFENSE FOR YOUR CHILD (with Alice McGrath)
[For elementary school-age boys & girls]
"...informative, readable book for family use..."
CHRISTIAN HOME & SCHOOL

DEFENSE TACTICS FOR LAW ENFORCEMENT
"...an excellent textbook for a basic course in self-defense..."
LAW BOOKS IN REVIEW

"...a practical tool for police academy programs, police programs
at the university level, and for the (individual) officer..."
THE POLICE CHIEF

SELF-DEFENSE NERVE CENTERS & PRESSURE POINTS
"...a practical guide to the most effective weaponless self-defense
using the least possible force..."　THE POLICE CHIEF

KUNG FU & TAI CHI: Chinese Karate and Classical Exercise
"...recommended for physical fitness collections."
LIBRARY JOURNAL

SOLO FORMS of Karate, Tai Chi, Aikido & Kung Fu (with Alice McGrath)
"...well-coordinated, step-by-step instructions...carefully captioned
photos...for personal enjoyment and exercise..." YA
American Library Association BOOKLIST

The author wishes to express his gratitude
and appreciation to:
RICHARD WINDISHAR, ELISE SIMMONS,
ROBERT SIMMONS, and DON PHILLIPS
for assisting him in demonstrating the
techniques in the photos.

To the memory of
T. SHOZO KUWASHIMA

CONTENTS

PREFACE

Judo is a relatively new sport. It was introduced in Japan in
the 1880's, the same decade that volleyball and basketball were
introduced in the United States. Jigaro Kano, a Japanese
educator and sport enthusiast, spent many years studying
specialties of the martial arts. From among them he synthesized
two new forms which he called *judo.*

For sport and physical development Professor Kano selected
throwing and grappling techniques. For self-defense he selected
hand and foot blows, holds, escapes and trips. He established
the Kodokan, a school for teaching judo. Beginning students
at the Kodokan were taught only the sport phase of judo--
throws and grappling. Advanced students were taught the
entirely different and separate techniques for self-defense. For
many years, continuing into the present, the word *judo* has
been used for both the sport form and the self-defense form of
the activity. Sometimes the terms *jujitsu* or *atemi waza* were
used to distinguish the self-defense activity from the sport of
judo. More often, *judo* and *jujitsu* were used interchangeably.
The resulting confusion delayed the acceptance of judo as a
legitimate sport. It also resulted in the sport techniques of

Jigaro Kano

judo being misperceived as self-defense. Professor Kano's own
writings and teachings made it clear that the sport of judo was
not intended for self-defense and his fervent hope was to have
judo recognized as a pure sport form.

Although he did not live to see it, Professor Kano's fondest
wish was realized when judo became an official Olympic Games
event. Today the word *judo* is increasingly understood to
designate the modern sport as it is practiced for fun and
physical fitness, and for competition up through Olympic
Games tournament.

*Professor Kano observes judo practice
at the Kodokan.*

ABOUT THE AUTHOR

Bruce Tegner was literally born to his vocation. Both his parents were professional teachers of judo and jujitsu and they began to teach him when he was two years old! His mother, June Tegner, was a remarkable woman who achieved the high rank of third degree black belt (*sandan*) under the tutelage of T. Shozo Kuwashima, an official representative of the Kodokan. When Jigaro Kano, the founder of judo, visited the United States, June Tegner traveled with his entourage and was later invited to study at the Kodokan. The Tegner family maintained a relationship with the Kodokan until after the death of Professor Kano and the beginning of World War II.

When he was eight years old, Mr. Tegner's instruction was taken up by Asian and European masters. In a subject area in which most individuals studied a single specialty of the martial arts, Tegner's background is exceptional. His education covered many styles of weaponless fighting and included instruction in sword and stick fighting. But judo remained his favored activity in his youth. He, too, studied with T. Shozo Kuwashima, and under Kuwashima's expert coaching achieved the rank of second black belt (*nidan*) at the age of seventeen--then the youngest second degree black belt on record in the United States. He then went on to become the California state judo champion in 1949.

June Tegner (seated right) and other judo students with T. Shozo Kuwashima (kneeling, middle).

Dear Bruce: *May 17th 1947*

It was great victory at Calif
Cavana club. I sincerely congra-
tulation for second Black Belt.

Yours
T. Shozo Kuwashima

NEW YORK DOJO (JUDO)

AUTHORIZED BY KODO KWAN, TOKYO

FOUNDED 1921

135 WEST 51st STREET

NEW YORK CITY

TELEPHONE COLUMBUS 5-8654

HONORARY ADVISORS

HON. RENZO SAWADA
CONSUL GENERAL OF JAPAN

CAPT. T. SAKURAI, I. J. N.
INSPECTOR, JAPANESE NAVY, N. Y.

COL. KASESHI BITO, I. J. A.
INSPECTOR JAPANESE ARMY, N. Y.

ANNOUNCEMENT

September 18, 1935

The Executive Committee of the New York Dojo is honored and happy to announce that beginning this week, we are to have the full-time and regular services of Professor Kuwashima, 5th Degree Kodokan, as Head Instructor.

Prof. Kuwaishima who has devoted his life to the study and further- ance of Judo, comes to us with a wealth of experience in teaching both Japanese and American peoples. Besides instructing in Mexico, being connected with Chicago University and training the Chicago police force, Prof. Kuswashima has conducted for the past fifteen years a Dojo in the latter city where more than 5,000 students have been enrolled in the study of Judo. During that time eighteen men who perservered received black belt degrees from the Kodokan and today maintain a Black Belt Degree Holders Association in Chicago.

Recently the Professor made a visit to Japan where honors were conferred by his college and the officials of the Kodokan in re- cognition of distinguished service rendered over the years and the high standards which he set in the furtherance of the art of Judo in America.

In welcoming Professor Kuwashima as Head Instructor, the Executive Committee wish to point out the almost unlimited possibilities in a city the size of New York for building this official branch of the Kodokan into one of the largest and most influential Dojos in the world. To that end we pledge to Professor Kuwashima our fullest co-operation and support.

Chairman of American Executive Committee

Bruce Tegner did not engage in competition after 1949, but devoted himself to research, writing, teaching, and teacher training. He had begun his teaching career while still a youngster, assisting in schools operated by his family. Professional activity was not a bar to competition in those days. In the U. S. Armed Forces, Mr. Tegner taught teachers of hand-to-hand combat, trained military police instructors and coached special services sport judo teams. He was also employed by the U. S. Government to train border patrol personnel and Treasury Department agents.

From 1952 to 1967 he operated a private school in Hollywood where he taught thousands of men, women and children, and was frequently called on for technical advice for movies and television programs. He instructed actors and invented spectacular fight scenes, and in several films he even took the role of villain, "losing" fights to actors whom he had trained.

Although Bruce Tegner was taught in a traditional manner, he introduced innovations in teaching procedures and concepts which were considered heretical at the time, but which have since been widely imitated and are now recognized as being consistent with modern concepts of health and physical education. He has devised many special courses, among them courses of practical self-defense which have been adopted in physical education classes throughout the world.

In addition to his continuing research and writing, he teaches in the Ventura County Community College District in California.

His many books in the subject field have been praised by professionals in physical education and by librarians. Some of his works have been published in Spanish, French, Portuguese, German and Dutch translations.

Bruce Tegner lives and works in Ventura, California.

INTRODUCTION

A TEACHING CONCEPT

In the traditional system of teaching judo, beginners are required to spend weeks or even months learning to fall safely. After intensive training and practice of *ukemi* (safety falls), the student is taught how to *receive* (to be thrown). Finally, the student is taught how to throw.

The old method is still widely used. For the highly motivated student under the tutelage of a skilled instructor, it works. For many people the old system has serious drawbacks. Teaching the falls before teaching the throws is a reversal of a logical order. It is more difficult to learn to be thrown than it is to learn how to throw. New students come to judo with the expectation of learning to throw; instead they are prevented from learning what they perceive to be the most interesting facet of judo. For a new student, being thrown is considerably less gratifying than being the thrower. Under the old system the incentive to heighten interest and promote enthusiasm is withheld.

Most students start judo practice because they are fascinated with the throwing techniques. Being made to practice the falls for a long time before being allowed to learn throwing techniques is discouraging to all but the most determined individuals.

I have developed an alternative method of teaching judo. It involves two concepts: Throws and falls are taught simultaneously, and there is a shift in roles and status.

By teaching throws *and* falls to beginning students, a high level of interest and motivation develop quickly.

In the traditional system, *tori*, the thrower, has a higher status than *uke*, who receives the throw. If the partner who takes the role of *uke* in practice is made to understand that his ability to be thrown is a highly valuable skill and contributes to faster progress for new students and if his ability to receive is acknowledged as a measure of advanced proficiency, the question of status is eliminated. In training practice, the concept of *uke* as "loser" is replaced by the concept of *uke* as advanced *judoka*, cooperating with the novice *tori* in an atmosphere of respect.

There is a significant safety factor in this method. An advanced player can be thrown by a beginner with relatively little danger of injury if the novice throws awkwardly or improperly.

As a coach in the United States Army I initiated the new method in training teams for judo competition. Later I adapted this method for teaching recreational sport judo with great success.

COLORED BELTS

When weaponless fighting was used in combat--when it was, literally, a martial art--there were no colored belts or ranks of proficiency. In a fight, the loser was injured or killed; the winner lived. Proficiency rating was introduced as these fighting skills became formalized, were modified for sport and exercise and were played in contest. Judo skill is now ranked by *degrees*, usually indicated by a colored belt. There is considerable variation in the requirements and procedures for advancing from the white belt of the novice to the black belt of the highly skilled player. There is no universal standard for promotion, nor is there a universal belt ranking system or color scheme. To make an accurate determination of the level of skill which a colored belt represents, one would have to be familiar with the requirements of the school, club or system in which it was awarded.

In some schools, promotion is by competition only, and advancement in degree is earned by winning in contest. Some schools emphasize formal demonstration of technique as the favored procedure for belt degree promotion. In other systems, degree promotions are achieved by a combination of formal demonstration and points won in contest. Instructors sometimes award belt degrees at their discretion; sometimes belt degrees are awarded by committees. Since few systems recognize the validity of belt degrees earned in other schools, a belt rank has real significance only within the system in which it is earned.

Belt ranks or grades are called *kyu* at the lower levels of proficiency and *dan* from the rank of first black belt and higher. The kyu ranks proceed from the lowest grade, sixth kyu, to the highest grade, first kyu. Rokkyu, sixth kyu, is given to the beginning student; other kyu grades are promotions from sixth through fifth, fourth, third, second and first kyu, ikkyu, an advanced rank commonly graded as brown belt. In the dan degrees, the lowest is shodan, or first degree black belt. Succeeding grades are nidan, second degree black belt; sandan, third degree black belt; yodan, fourth degree black belt; godan, fifth degree black belt, and on up to twelfth degree black belt. It is uncommon for players to earn a belt degree above fifth dan in contest or tournament; higher ranks are usually honorary.

Color schemes for belt ranks, as well as the specific requirements for promotion, vary throughout the world. The original scheme of progression from white to brown to black to red to white (symbolizing a full circle, or completion), has been modified and colors have been introduced to rank proficiency with intermediate step levels from white to black.

In the United States, advancement from white to green to brown to black belt is common. In Canada, South America and Europe, there is a wide range of belt rank systems, including one which goes from white to yellow to orange to green to blue to brown to black.

One rule is absolute: A player may not rank himself! Self-ranking would make all proficiency ratings meaningless. No matter how hard a student has worked, or how sincere he is, he may not grant himself a belt degree. This is no different than in other fields of study. An individual is not allowed the privilege of giving himself a driver's license, a high school diploma or a teaching credential.

In traditional judo, players are matched in contest solely on the basis of belt rank, with separate classes for women and children. In modern judo, players are *not* matched according to belt rank, but through elimination matches and in weight classes.

The Olympic Games judo committee recognizes a number of judo associations whose members are permitted to wear their rank belts in contest; other players must wear the white belt of the novice, regardless of their level of skill. The recognition of an organization means only that there is a formal relationship, but it does not mean the judo clubs or groups without "official" recognition are incapable of producing tournament judo players. Independent schools and clubs enter players at the highest level of international tournament judo, which means that those individuals have had excellent training.

It is highly unlikely that individuals practicing on their own could achieve a high level of proficiency. Tournament skill is achieved through very hard work, good coaching by an experienced judo instructor and the opportunity to work out with other good players.

The belt degree requirements which follow are those I have used, with some modifications, for many years. They are given as an example of a belt-ranking system and should be regarded as guideline information. Clubs and schools may follow this or a similar system of ranking.

JUDO UNIFORM – GI

The Japanese name for the judo uniform is *gi*, pronounced *gee* with the "g" as in "go."

The jacket of the judo gi is made of double-weave, reinforced heavy cotton. The front opening, all along the edge and around the neck, is bound with extra reinforcement to withstand grasping and pulling. There is no collar or lapel on a judo uniform; when an instruction in the text refers to "collar" or "lapel" it is to be interpreted as meaning that area of the front opening which is around the neck in the collar area, or at the chest at lapel height.

The sleeves of the jacket should extend a little more than halfway between the elbow and wrist. The pant legs must extend down a little more than halfway between the knees and ankles. The belt goes around the body twice and is tied in front with a square knot.

BEGINNER – ROKKYU

The beginning judo student is designated *rokkyu* and wears a white belt. In this phase of instruction the beginner learns the fundamental rules of safety, the basic principles of judo, and then begins the study and practice of techniques and procedures required for advancement to *gokkyu*.

ADVANCED WHITE BELT – GOKKYU

REQUIREMENTS

First ten falls
Four throws
    Kickback throw--osoto gari
    Basic hip throw--ogoshi
    Hip throw--tsuri komi goshi
    Sweeping-foot throw--de ashi harai
    Kneeblock wheeling throw--hiza guruma
Mat work
    Side shoulder hold
        Three variations
    Cross-body hold
        Three variations
Give-and-take sparring

In formal demonstration, the student exhibits reasonable proficiency in the above techniques and demonstrates give-and-take sparring. Then he is designated *gokkyu*, still wearing a white belt, and begins to work on the requirements for advancement to the next degree.

GREEN BELT – YONKYU

REQUIREMENTS

Falls
  Leaping falls
Throws
  Straight-leg throw--tai otoshi
  Inside sweeping-foot throw--ko uchi gari
  Arm-around-neck hip throw--koshi guruma
  Shoulder throw--seoinage
Counter throws
Combination throws
Mat work
  Top-body hold
    Three variations
  Straddling-body hold
    Three variations
Contest--randori

The candidate for advancement to green belt degree demonstrates the ability to perform the advanced falls in a formal manner. Then the four throws are demonstrated in a formal manner, with the candidate rated on throwing ability and receiving ability. Finally, to earn the rank, the candidate must win a point in contest (randori) against two different players at his level of skill. In randori, the candidate should show the ability to use counters, combination throws and to apply mat work techniques.

THIRD DEGREE BROWN BELT – SANKYU

Green belt rank students will now begin to learn and practice techniques, strategy and tactics to prepare for advancement to the next level.

REQUIREMENTS

Throws
  Side sweeping-foot throw--okuri ashi harai
  Innercut throw--o chi gari
  Outercut throw--ko soto gake
  Sweeping-thigh throw--harai goshi

Mat work
  Holding
    Reverse side-shoulder hold
    Arm-and-head shoulder hold
    Kneeling side-shoulder hold
  Arm locks
    Bent-arm lock, in
    Straight-arm lock, out, with arm pressure
  Chokes
    Crossed-arm choke
    Front sliding choke
  Contest--randori

In addition to formal demonstration of the new techniques, the candidate for advancement to sankyu will have to win one point in contest against two different opponent players. Players at this level will be expected to show considerable improvement in skill and style of randori and to exhibit more sophisticated tactics of offensive and defensive play.

SECOND DEGREE BROWN BELT — NIKYU

REQUIREMENTS

Throws
  Arm-around shoulder hip throw--ippon seoi nage
  Back sweeping-foot throw--ko soto gari
  Upper innercut throw--uchi mate
  Lateral sacrificing throw--uki waza
  Circle throw--tomoe nage
Mat work
  Arm locks
    Straight-arm lock, up, with leg pressure
    Straight-arm lock with hip pressure
    Straight-arm lock into body
  Chokes
    Knuckle choke
    One-arm cross choke
  Contest--randori

Candidates for nikyu degree demonstrate formal techniques showing improvement in technical skill. They must earn one point in contest with two different opponent players. Style and skill are expected to be on a higher level than for the previous grade.

1. *"Easy" judo is judo play with seeming effortlessness. At the black belt level, judo throwing has the appearance of being easy; the skill is acquired through years of hard work.*

FIRST DEGREE BROWN BELT — IKKYU

REQUIREMENTS

Throws
    Pulling-down straight-leg throw--uki otoshi
    Lifting sweeping-foot throw--harai tsurikomi ashi
    Spring-leg throw--hana goshi
    Inside lateral sacrifice throw--sumi gaesha
Mat work
    Arm locks
        Straight-arm lock with body lever
        Straight-arm lock with leg lever
        Combination straight-arm lock/bent-arm lock
        Rear bent-arm lock
    Chokes
        Loop choke
        Rear forearm choke
        Rear neck lock
Contest--randori

Since this is the highest brown belt degree, the candidates are expected to demonstrate excellence in formal demonstration, and to use offensive/defensive tactics utilizing a wide variety of techniques to win the required two points against two different opponents in randori.

FIRST BLACK BELT — SHODAN

In traditional judo, the black belt was considered the significant belt rank. In modern judo, the preceding steps leading to black belt are important grades. In tournament play, many brown belt players exhibit excellent style and technique. But it is the black belt which all serious judoka aspire to earn.

REQUIREMENTS

Throws
    Crab claw throw--kani waza
    Binding throw--soto makikomi
    Back hip throw--ura goshi
    Shouldering throw--kata juruma
    Rear hip throw--ushiro goshi
Chokes
    Rear sliding choke
    Under-and-over arm choke
Formal routine of throwing--naga no kata
Contest--randori

The candidates for black belt have three demonstrations to perform--the new throws, the mat work and the 15-throw formal routine. They are expected to show near perfection in the formal demonstrations. The contest points won in matches against two different opponent players should reveal a highly developed individual style of play appropriate for advancement to the level of black belt expert.

SAFE JUDO PRACTICE

When the rules for safe practice are understood and observed, there is a relatively low incidence of accidental injury in judo practice.

The instructor, coach or group leader is responsible for teaching and enforcing the observance of safety rules.

DO NOT ALLOW yourself to be thrown until you have been taught to fall safely. DO NOT THROW anyone who has not been trained to receive.

Throwing and falling should be practiced on a mat or padded floor. Originally, straw (tatami) mats were the standard playing surface and there are clubs which still use them. Wrestling mats are currently used for tournament and randori. Care should be taken to keep the playing surface clean and free of metal fasteners, rips, and ridges.

FIRST AID & MEDICAL RESPONSIBILITY

If you engage in group practice, even on a friendly, informal basis, you should have the telephone number of a doctor or hospital on hand so that you do not lose valuable time in the event of an emergency. If you give some thought to this before-hand, you can avoid acting in a panic and you can assure the injured person the best chance of needed care.

Advanced judo players should be familiar with modern tech-niques of first aid which apply to possible judo practice accidents: sprains, dislocations, fractures, and unconscious-ness. Most communities offer free courses in current methods of first aid.

A doctor should be in attendance at any open contest.

TAPPING FOR RELEASE OR STOP ACTION

Tapping twice is the signal for "stop" or "release." It is a prime rule of safety in judo practice. Tapping, as in photo 2, is the best and fastest way to effect release or stop the action.

Tapping is more effective than a vocal signal because there are times when a verbal request would be difficult--when practicing choking techniques, for example. In a room full of students practicing, a verbal signal might not be easy to hear. You can also tap the mat as a signal to stop.

When the tapping signal is given, IMMEDIATE RELEASE or stop action is required. It is dangerous and discourteous to maintain a hold or to continue any technique if your partner taps.

It is unnecessary to endure needless pain in the practice of judo. The moment you feel that a mat work technique has been applied correctly and is hurting you, tap for release! If you feel that a throw is being applied with needless force, tap to stop the action.

*2. Two quick taps
your partner can
feel is the signal for
"stop" or "release."
Or you can tap the
mat.*

ROUGH PRACTICE

You should decline to practice with any partner who persistently
uses force rather than skill. Rough play is discourteous, unsafe
and incompetent. A practice partner who does not release
immediately at the tapping signal, who uses illegal tactics such
as hitting or kicking, or whose general style is rough, is sub-
jecting you to unnecessary possibility of injury.

*It is customary for judo
players to bow when they
enter the training area, and
then they bow to the teacher.*

*3. At the beginning and end
of a practice session, they bow
to each other.*

*Before leaving, they bow to
the teacher and to the training
area.*

TORI/UKE

Tori is the person who throws, or who applies the technique.
Uke is the person who receives the action. *Tori* and *thrower*
are used interchangeably in the text. *Receiver* and *uke* are
used interchangeably. Unless otherwise indicated, the "you"
in the instruction is always tori.

VOCABULARY

There is no standard English-language translation of the judo vocabulary. Japanese words, in italics, are sounded with equal stress on all syllables. "Ei" sounds like "ay" in hay; "ai" sounds like "I"; "i" sounds like "ee"; "e" sounds like the "e" in end; "g" is hard, as in go.

atemi waza. Hand and foot blows (not allowed in sport judo)

BY-CHANCE. A tactic applied as the opportunity presents itself; not planned

COURTESY THROW. An unopposed throw in judo practice (not in contest). A gesture of deference to rank; a lower grade player allows the courtesy throw to a higher degree partner

dan. The black belt ranks

    shodan. 1st degree

    nidan. 2nd degree

    sandan. 3rd degree

    yodan. 4th degree

    godan. 5th degree

dojo. The judo practice gym

FORMS. Rehearsed patterns of series of movements; groups of throws, matwork, and counterthrows

gi. The judo uniform

GIVE-AND-TAKE PRACTICE. Partners alternate throwing or practice; no resistance is made

GROUNDWORK. Grappling; mat work

hajime. Start the match

hansoku. Illegal contest tactic

hiki wake. Draw match

ippon. Full point

jikan. Time

judoka. Judo player

kachi. Win

kansetsu waza. Locking techniques

kata. See "forms"

katame waza. Grappling techniques

ki ai. A shout used in judo at the instant of critical action

Kodokan. School of judo founded by Jigaro Kano

kuzushi. Breaking opponent's balance

kyu. Belt rank levels below black belt; the lowest kyu grade is sixth kyu (rokkyu); the highest is first kyu (ikkyu)

MAT WORK. Grappling techniques

nage waza. Throwing techniques

ne waza. Mat work
obi. Belt
osaekomi. Holding
randori. Free-style play
RECEIVER. Person who is thrown; in mat work, the person on whom the hold is taken
rei. Bow
SACRIFICE, OR SACRIFICING THROW. A throw in which the thrower puts himself on the mat as he throws
sensei. Teacher
shiai. Contest
shime waza. Choking techniques
shinpan. Judge, referee
sogo gachi. Compound win
sono mama. Stop; stop the match; do not move
STANDING WORK. Throws or chokes
STEMI. A derivative of *sutemi*; to throw oneself; leaping falls
STIFF-ARMING. Holding arms rigid to prevent being thrown
sutemi waza. See "sacrifice"
toketa. Hold broken
tori. The person who throws; in mat work, the person who applies the technique
uke. The person on whom a technique is applied; same as "receiver"
ukemi. Safety falls; breakfalls
waza ari. Almost a full point
yoshi. Carry on

The Japanese names for specific throws are given where the throws are taught. See also: Index.

4   5

KICKBACK THROW — O SOTO GARI

4. The beginning practice position is as shown. Both players grip cloth at the partner's lapel with the right hand and under the partner's sleeve with the left hand.

5. As you take a deep step with your left foot, placing it next to your partner's right foot, tilt him into off-balance position with circular arm movement, pushing around and down with your right hand and arm, and pulling with your left hand.

6. As the wheeling arm movement is applied, swing your right leg up . . .

7. . . . and kick his right leg, calf-to-calf. The throw is completed by a continuous wheeling arm movement and follow-through of the swinging leg.

8. The follow-through is shown as tori kicks uke's leg up . . .

9. . . . and releases his right hand grip to allow uke to fall safely.

6

7

8

9

10. The ending position is shown. For practice, uke maintains his right hand grip and tori maintains his left hand grip to ease uke's fall.

A common error made by beginners is to attempt to *push* the leg. The swinging leg action which is correct for this throw does not depend on force, but on timing. If the calf-to-calf kick is timed so that it hits uke's leg when it is not weight-bearing, very little strength is needed to do it successfully. Arm and leg movement must work together; even if you successfully swing uke's leg out from under him, he cannot be thrown easily if his weight is well balanced on the other leg. If you feel that you are *wrestling* him down, you have not applied properly coordinated canting and kicking actions.

BODY THROW RECEIVING

The throw which follows--the basic hip throw--is more difficult to receive than is the preceding throw because uke moves through a longer and higher arc. If you are learning to receive the hip throw, tori should use the arm-around-the-waist version to ease your fall. He will further assist you by dragging his arm across your back as you go over his body and he will maintain his left hand grip on your sleeve throughout. As his arm drags across your back, release your left hand grip and drag it across tori's back as you position your left hand to slap the mat. Your ending should correspond to the basic side fall. Timing is critical; if you slap too soon or too late, your slap will not absorb impact and you will fall heavily onto your side or back.

When each of the partners drags his hand across his partner's back, it slows the throw and makes it easier to receive. When throwing a partner who is learning to receive, tori maintains his left hand cloth grip and pulls up to ease the fall. Uke maintains his right hand cloth grip. In randori practice (free-style play) tori releases both hand grips to allow uke to take a safe fall and to avoid being dragged onto the mat.

WEIGHT DISTRIBUTION

To execute the body throws properly, you must learn how to support the weight of a partner who is at least as heavy as you are. Although the execution of the throw in free style will put uke's weight on you for an instant, it is a critical instant. What happens in that instant will determine whether you can complete a successful, crisp throw, or whether uke will slide off your back.

11. It is possible to support the weight of a partner who is considerably heavier than you are if weight distribution is correct and if your stance is strong and well-balanced.

To take your partner to balance, stand with your feet about shoulder width apart and your knees slightly bent. Your partner stands behind you. Without moving your legs, bend your upper body sharply to the left from the waist only. Put your arm around your partner's waist or neck and topple him onto your back and hip as you press upward with your hip. Do not attempt to *lift* him with your arms.

The exact position of your legs will vary according to the size of your partner. You will bend your knees more when balancing a shorter person than when taking a taller person to balance. Practice this procedure until you can easily support someone your size or larger without losing your balance.   **11**

Check for the correct technique:

Are your knees bent at the correct angle? If your legs are too straight or you are squatting too low you will not be able to support the weight.

Are your knees apart, as shown? If your knees collapse inward, your stance becomes weak.

Is ONLY your upper body flexed to the left? Unless you bend from the waist and your right hip juts out markedly, you will not be in position to support the weight.

Are you pressing upward with your hip? This action assists both weight-bearing and throwing.

You should be able to take your partner to balance easily before you practice the body throws.

12   13

BASIC HIP THROW — OGOSHI

12. Begin in the standard position. Tori wears the gray gi.

13. Start the back-in pivot, sliding your left foot counterclockwise so that your feet are parallel, with the toes pointing in opposite directions. Keep your right foot in place and maintain your hand grips. Your body turns to follow the movement of your left foot.

14. Complete the pivot by turning counterclockwise as you take a step with your right foot to place it in front of uke's right foot. Both your feet are directly in front of his feet. Without changing your left-hand grip, slide your right arm around his waist. Your upper body is bent sharply to your left; your knees are bent so that your right hip is positioned against uke's thigh.

15. To apply the throw, pull around and down with your left hand as you lift with your right arm and turn your body to the left, springing up to straighten your legs as you turn.

The foregoing is the basic body throw. When you can perform the mechanics of this throw easily and smoothly, you will find the other body throws relatively simple to learn. Use the arm-around-the-waist version until you can easily balance your partner.

This version of the throw is a practice procedure. It is not a contest throw. However, a variation of this version may be used in contest. Since you may, under limited conditions, grip uke's belt to assist a throw, you could reach around, grip his belt and apply the throw.

14   15

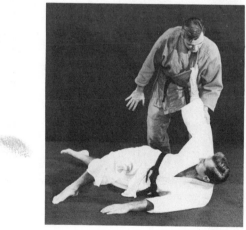

16

16. Uke falls in the basic side fall position on the left side, slapping with his left hand and right foot.

17

18

19

20

SWEEPING-FOOT THROW — DE ASHI HARAI

Partners start in the standard position. Tori is shown right.

17. Using a wheeling arm motion, tilt uke toward your right side, shifting his weight onto his left foot. This action puts him in weak balance on his right side.

18. Catch uke's right instep with the bottom of your left foot . . .

19. . . . and as you sweep his right foot out from under him . . .

20. . . . reverse the direction of your wheeling arm movement, taking him around and down.

Timing is critical. If you sweep too soon or too late you will not be able to raise his foot with an easy movement. You cannot sweep the foot when it is bearing weight. To perfect your timing, move about on the mat with your partner and practice the sweeping action. This can be done with many repetitions, without actually throwing. If you can easily apply the sweep so that your partner is completely off balance, you will enhance your ability to execute the throw.

The sweeping-foot throw can be done with equal ease from the right or the left side and it can be applied if your opponent is moving toward you or pulling away. It combines with many other throws for flexible contest use.

21   22

STRAIGHT-LEG THROW — TAI OTOSHI

Players start in the standard position. Tori is shown right.

21. Point your left foot away from uke . . .

22. . . . and shift your weight onto your left leg as you lock your right ankle at his right ankle . . .

23   24

23. ... and, without hesitation, pull him around and down with a wheeling arm and body action, keeping your right leg firmly in place.

Be sure your right leg is fully extended and straight. Note that uke is pulled close into your chest, around and down. The ending requires continuous arm and body twisting.

24. A beginning receiver might trip around tori's leg. A skilled player will fling his legs up and over to take a better fall.

ARM-AROUND-NECK HIP THROW — KOSHI GURUMA

From the standard starting position, pivot to place yourself in front of uke, and . . .

25 26

25. . . . as you pivot, slide your arm around his neck.

26. Take to balance, using a wheeling-around movement of your right arm and upper body. Note that you can practice throws without completing them, if you balance your partner as shown here, and then allow him to return to the starting position. Since it is obvious that the throw *can* be completed when you have come to this point in the action, you can practice the essential technique with a great many repetitions without requiring uke to take the fall.

27

27. As the throw is completed, tori's right arm follows through with the wheeling, levering action until uke's weight actually leaves tori's hip.

28

29

30

KNEEBLOCK WHEELING THROW — HIZA GURUMA

28. From the standard starting position, break uke's balance forward by pulling him toward you, and shift your weight onto your right foot . . .

29. . . . and place the bottom of your left foot at his right knee and wheel sharply around and down with your arms as you lift with the left leg . . .

30. . . . to complete the throw. Your right leg should be slightly bent to keep you in good balance.

31

HIP THROW — TSURI KOMI GOSHI

31. The hip throw used in randori and as it is performed for formal demonstration is applied in the same manner as the basic or training version, with the exception that tori does not put his arm around uke's waist to throw, but maintains his right hand grip and levers up under uke's left armpit with his right elbow to assist the throw.

32

33

ARM-AROUND-SHOULDER HIP THROW — IPPON SEOI NAGE

32. As you pivot into position, maintain your left hand grip, but drop your right arm . . .

33. . . . and regrip high on his right arm at the shoulder and apply the throw.

34

SHOULDER THROW – SEOI NAGE

The body action in this throw is the same as in the basic hip throw.

34. As the pivot is executed, maintain both hand grips, but place your right elbow into uke's right armpit.

As the throw is applied, use your right elbow for a wheeling action, up, around and then down, to assist the body action.

Because there is no change in hand position, this version can be applied more quickly than the preceding hip throws. As tori positions his right arm, it helps him get into a good, low, throwing stance.

Uke takes a high fall and must be a skilled receiver before being thrown vigorously.

LATERAL SACRIFICING THROW – UKI WAZA

Players begin in the standard position. Tori is shown left.

35. Pivoting on the ball of your left foot, move your body to uke's right side as you place your right foot onto his left instep.

36. Pulling with both arms, bend your left leg to lower yourself onto the mat . . .

35

36

37

38

37. . . . and continue pulling with your arms and body to trip him forward, assisting this action by thrusting upward with your right foot . . .

38. . . . releasing both of your hand grips in time to allow uke to receive safely.

Tori must be out of the line of fall, or uke will fall onto him. It is essential to allow uke to take his fall without restraint so that he can roll out, otherwise he might be pulled onto his head.

39   40

41

BACK SWEEPING-FOOT THROW — KO SOTO GARI

39. From the facing starting position, take a step back, clock-wise, with your right foot so that you are at uke's side.

40. As you tilt him back, sweep the back of his foot with the bottom of your left foot . . .

41. . . . and follow through with the sweep to raise his leg, and use a lively wheeling arm action, around and down, to complete the throw.

42

43

44

INNERCUT THROW — O UCHI GARI

42. Tori is shown left. From the standard starting position, use arm movement to wheel uke toward your left side, as you hook his left leg at the knee.

43. With his left leg captured and locked firmly with your bent leg, wheel him clockwise, using arm and body motion.

44. The throw is assured.

Now release the captured leg and follow through with lively arm and body movement. The timing of the leg release is critical; if it is released too soon, uke can regain his balance; if it is released too late, it prevents a good fall, and you might be pulled down onto the mat.

This throw can be done with equal ease on the right or left side and when players are moving in any direction.

45   46

47

CIRCLE THROW — TOMOE NAGE

45. Tori is shown left. Take a step forward with your left foot . . .

46. . . . and then take a little hop on your left foot to get in very close to uke and place your right foot at his belt, pulling forward with both arms . . .

47. . . . and sit down onto the mat, continuing the arm action and assisting his forward movement with your bent right leg.

Release uke in time to receive safely and properly. Do not stiff-leg as you pull him forward, or he will fall onto you.

SWEEPING-THIGH THROW — HARAI GOSHI

This is an excellent throw for a taller player to use against an equal or shorter opponent; it is very difficult for a smaller man to use against a taller player of approximately equal skill.

48. From the standard starting position, begin a wheeling arm action as you pivot in . . .

48

49

50

49. . . . with your back to uke. As you pivot, shift your weight onto your left leg, somewhat bent to bear weight, and continue the wheeling arm action as you position your extended right leg . . .

50. . . . for the sweeping action which, combined with follow-through of the wheeling arms, completes the throw. Use a springing-up hip action to assist and accelerate the throw.

To avoid being pulled off balance, prepare to take a good, low "T" stance as uke goes over.

PULLING DOWN STRAIGHT-LEG THROW — UKI OTOSHI

51, 52. From the standard beginning position, pull uke with both hands as you bend your left leg and lower yourself to the mat onto your left knee, continuing to pull . . .

53, 54. . . . and, without hesitation, extend your right leg and place it ankle-to-ankle at his right ankle, following through with arm movement, in a wheeling action, to take uke over your leg.

Although you can *trip* uke over your extended leg if you brace your toes firmly into the mat, a better throw is applied if you use lively, continuous arm movement to *wheel* him over.

With experience, tori can leap from a standing position into the position shown in photo 53. When you are learning this throw you should take the interim step in photo 52.

55

56

57

OUTERCUT THROW — KO SOTO GAKE

55. Tori is shown right. As uke is tilted backward, hook a leg around from the outside, as shown . . .

56. . . . and, locking the captured leg with your bent leg, wheel uke back and around . . .

57. . . . and down as you pull forward on the captured leg.

The wheeling arm action must be lively and continuous. Follow through with the leg hook. The photos show the outercut throw being applied with tori's left leg hooking uke's right leg; it can be used with equal ease on either side.

58   59

LIFTING SWEEPING-FOOT THROW — HARAI TSURIKOMI ASHI

58. From the standard starting position, sidestep with your right foot and point it toward uke, as shown. Pull him forward and up onto his toes as you place your left foot at his right ankle.

59. The throw is effected by pulling uke into your chest with both arms and then changing into a wheeling around-and-down arm action, while following through with the foot sweep so that uke's locked leg is raised as he falls.

60

61

62

INSIDE LATERAL SACRIFICE THROW — SUMI GAESHA

60. The beginning action of the throw is the same as for the basic lateral sacrifice throw.

61. As uke is wheeled around to your left side, place your right instep at the inside of his leg and follow through . . .

62. . . . with a lively, lifting action of your right leg to assist the throw.

63

64

65

UPPER INNERCUT THROW — UCHI MATA

Start in the standard position.

63. Using a wheeling arm action, break uke's balance and begin a back-in pivot.

64. After completing the pivot, swing your leg back and up, vigorously, hitting uke's upper inner thigh with the back of your thigh. As the leg sweeps, the wheeling arm motion is continued.

65. The throw is completed by following through with the sweeping leg and the arm movement and is assisted by a twisting body action.

With practice, tori can execute this throw so that uke goes over in a high arc. Uke must be a skilled receiver.

SPRING-LEG THROW — HANE GOSHI

The basic actions of the sweeping-thigh throw, the spring-leg throw and the upper innercut throw are similar. Although tori's leg is bent in the application of the spring-leg throw and it is straight in the other two throws, the body action and the wheeling arm movements are alike in all three throws.

66

67

66. Tori uses a back-in pivot to get into position.

67,68. As you begin the sweeping-lifting action with your bent leg, start the wheeling arm movement which will take uke off balance and over.

This throw can also be applied against both legs, taking uke over in a higher arc if he is a skilled receiver.

68

69   70

71

INSIDE SWEEPING-FOOT THROW — KO UCHI GARI

69. Shift uke so that he is bearing weight on his left foot.

70. With the bottom of your right foot, sweep his right foot at the ankle, outward and forward as you . . .

71. . . . complete the throw with follow-through wheeling arm movement as the swept foot is raised.

72

73

74

75

SIDE SWEEPING-FOOT THROW — OKURI ASHI HARAI

72. Tilt uke so that most of his weight is on his left foot.

73. Sweep uke's raised foot with your left foot.

74. As you raise the swept foot, reverse your tilting action to shift his weight toward his raised foot.

75. Both his feet are raised by the sweeping action and then you wheel him down and around with arm action. Follow-through in the leg sweep is essential for a good throw.

76

77

78

79

REAR HIP THROW — USHIRO GOSHI

This technique is used chiefly as a counterthrow.

76, 77. For instance, your opponent, shown right, attempts a
body throw, which puts his back toward you and you respond by
blocking his attempt by bending his knee with your knee and
squatting . . .

78, 79. . . . so that your thighs are below his thighs and you pull
him back, off balance, and effect the throw by pulling back on
his upper body as you straighten your body to lift and bounce his
lower body up. Release uke so that he can take a safe fall.

80

81

82

BACK HIP THROW — URA GOSHI

80. From the standard starting position, take a deep step with your left foot . . .

81. . . . and then another deep step with your right foot so that you are behind uke. As you step, push him back to break his balance. Bend your knees and lean your upper body sharply to the left; place your hips just below his hips.

82. As you wheel him around and down with your arms, twist your body sharply to take him over.

83   84

BINDING THROW — SOTO MAKIKOMI

This throw is not always permitted in contest. If tori falls onto his opponent, there is a possibility of injury. Because body weight is important in the application of this throw, it is highly impractical for a lighter player to attempt against a heavier opponent.

83. Tori is shown right. From the starting position, pivot on the ball of your left foot as you turn your body counterclockwise and pull uke's right arm forward . . .

84. . . . as you step around counterclockwise with your right foot so that your back is at uke's right side. As you turn, pull his right arm with your left hand, release your right hand grip and bring your right arm over the captured arm.

85   86

85. The throw is effected by using body weight to take uke down to the mat and you go down onto the mat with him. You lean back as you raise your right leg and fall.

86. For the correct ending position, uke falls on his back, his left hand free to slap the mat. You must take care not to fall onto his chest, but fall at his side, absorbing the impact of your fall with your forearm.

87

88

89

90

CRAB CLAW THROW — KANI WAZA

87, 88. Take a clockwise step with your right foot and shift your
weight toward your right side and release your right hand grip
and position your left leg across uke's thighs . . .

89, 90. . . . and place your right hand on the mat as you spring
up to place your right leg behind his knees. Pull back sharply
with your left hand, twisting your body so that you fall on your
back, releasing your left hand grip to allow uke to fall safely.

Some systems of judo do not allow this throw in lower degree
contest because of the possibility of leg injury if the throw is
not skillfully executed.

91

92

SHOULDERING THROW —

KATA GURUMA

93

91. Break uke's balance forward . . .

92. . . . and, keeping your upper body erect, squat as you place your right foot between his feet. Pull him with your left hand. With your right hand grip cloth at the back of his right leg . . .

93. . . . toppling him across your shoulders with a wheeling arm movement assisted by a springing-up straightening of your legs.

This throw requires a high level of receiving skill and should not be attempted unless your practice partner is proficient in taking the falls.

94   95

BALANCE

94. In a natural standing position there is fairly strong balance from side to side. If you push at your partner's side, as shown, you will feel considerable resistance.

95. In the same natural stance, your partner is vulnerable to the front and back. Using only your fingertips, you can topple him forward off balance with hardly any resistance.

You could topple him back off balance as easily, using fingertip pressure.

96. One-point balance is the most vulnerable stance. Balanced on one foot, there is weakness in every direction. Very light pressure is required to maneuver an opponent player into off-balance throwing position.

96

97   98

"T" STANCE

The strongest solid balance is the "T" stance, which is used in many physical activities, including fencing. The "T" stance permits flexible movement while it provides resistance to being pulled or pushed off balance.

The "T" stance is taken with one foot advanced, toes pointing forward, the rear foot at a 90-degree angle. If you were to draw your feet together in this position, they would form a "T."

97. In the "T" stance there is maximum stability from side to side . . .

98. . . . and there is maximum stability from front to back.

99. When practicing any throw which might pull you off balance or when practicing any technique which makes you vulnerable to loss of balance, finish in a strong "T" stance, with your knees slightly bent to lower your center of gravity.

99

100   101

CANTING AND TILTING

Canting and tilting are methods of maneuvering your opponent
so that he is off balance or in weak balance. Canting and tilting
are primarily accomplished with arm action, but you can use
body movement to help twist or tilt your opponent. Very good
players use subtle arm movements as they move about the mat,
gently shifting, guiding and maneuvering the opponent into
position for a throwing attempt.

100. You can tilt your opponent by pulling him forward . . .

101. . . . or by pushing him back.

102. Canting is a twisting action. Here the right player is
pulling toward himself with his left hand, and pushing with
his right hand. The left player is in weak balance and vulnerable to a throwing attempt.

103. Apply continuous and gradual traction to pull your
opponent up onto the balls of his feet and forward, off
balance . . .

104. . . . and then cant him around, to the side.

Partners should take turns practicing the canting and tilting
arm actions. At first, practice these procedures from a standstill.
You will soon learn the feel of armwork maneuvering and realize
how significant armwork can be in applying judo throws. After
you have practiced armwork from a standstill, practice the same
maneuvering actions as you slide about on the mat.

102

103

104

105

105. Your partner is in position to be thrown when you have canted him into weak balance. To complete the throw you must follow through with body-wheeling arm movement. Practice the follow-through arm movements, wheeling your partner around to your left and around to your right.

FOOTWORK

Normal walking steps are not appropriate for judo. Walking puts you into one-point balance too much of the time. In one-point balance you are vulnerable to being thrown.

Instead of walking, use a gliding-sliding movement on the balls of your feet. Keep your weight distributed equally on both feet as much as possible. Keep your feet at least six inches apart. Except in preparation for applying a throw, do not cross your feet or lift them. Maintain maximum contact with the mat for strong, solid balance.

Judo footwork as described above lets you move easily and quickly. It allows you to maneuver the opponent player without putting you into vulnerable positions.

From the standard beginning position, bend your knees slightly and practice gliding-sliding movement in all directions. Try to avoid lifting your feet from the mat as you and your partner maneuver, pull, push, cant and move forward, around and back.

106

107

PIVOTS

FIRST PIVOT

106. Partners start from the standard practice starting position.

107. Slide your left foot in a half circle counterclockwise, placing it in front of your partner's left foot, with your toes pointing away from him. Your right foot stays in place, but your body will turn to follow the pivot.

108. Without moving your left foot, turn your body and step with your right foot, placing it in front of your partner's right foot. When you complete the pivot, both your feet should be directly in front of your partner's feet. You are somewhat crouched, as shown. You maintain your hand grips throughout the pivot.

108

109

110

SECOND PIVOT

109. From the starting position, step across in front of yourself with your right foot, placing it in front of your partner's right foot, with weight only on the ball of the foot.

110. Pivoting on the ball of your right foot, turn your body counterclockwise to place yourself directly in front of your partner, your feet in front of his feet. You maintain your hand grips as you pivot. You are slightly crouched, as shown.

111   112

THIRD PIVOT

111. From the starting position, step across in front of yourself with your left foot, placing it in front of your partner's left foot, with weight only on the ball of the foot.

112. Pivoting on the ball of your left foot, turn your body counterclockwise and place yourself directly in front of your partner, as shown.

113   114

FOURTH PIVOT

113. The starting position is facing uke with your left foot in front of his left foot.

114. Pivoting on the ball of your left foot, turn counterclockwise to place yourself directly in front of him.

115   116

FIFTH PIVOT

115. The starting position is facing uke with your right foot in front of his right foot.

116. Pivoting on the ball of your right foot, back in, turning counterclockwise, to place yourself directly in front of him.

117   118

SIXTH PIVOT

117, 118. From the starting position, take a short step back away from uke without releasing your hand grips, and . . .

119. ...spring up from the balls of both feet, leap and twist your body counterclockwise and ...

120. ...land directly in front of him, in position to throw.

SEVENTH PIVOT

121. From the standard starting position, take a short step back from uke, without releasing your hand grips. Spring up from the ball of your left foot, as you bend your right leg and twist your body . . .

122. . . . to finish in position to apply a spring-leg throw. You can also use the one-foot leaping pivot with your right leg extended, in position to apply a straight-leg throw.

123

124

TRAINING BALL

123, 124. This is a simple, effective training procedure to improve sweeping foot actions. Partners sweep a ball to each other using the same motion as is used in the foot-sweep throws.

125   126

LEG ACTION WITH BAG

Improvise this training aid by filling a duffel bag or canvas laundry bag with wood shavings, sawdust or rags. Do not use sand.

This training practice is for improving your ability to apply the correct leg action for the lifting and sweeping throws. You can develop technique and strength in solo practice and you can engage in much longer practice sessions than you could with a partner.

You will experience the feeling of applying the leg action against a weighted, moving object, which is useful for contest work.

125, 126. Holding the bag out in front of you, practice the foot sweeps. Alternate practice with right and left feet. Emphasize the follow-through action; sweep the bag up high.

127, 128. Holding the bag somewhat behind you, practice the action of kicking as though calf-to-calf in the manner of the kick-back throw.

129, 130. Holding the bag with one hand, practice the leg lifting action as though for the spring-leg throw.

127

128

129

130

ARM WORK & PIVOT EXERCISE

A practice procedure which you can use to enhance the techniques of arm work can be done with a partner or by yourself.

The equipment is a piece of rope about one meter (approximately three feet) long. If you work with a partner, you can take turns holding the rope. In solo practice, improvise a way of securing the rope (perhaps with a pulley) so that it moves easily and so that you can exert considerable pull.

131. Hold one end of the rope as though you were gripping your opponent at the lapel and the other end as though you were gripping cloth at the sleeve. You are simulating the standard throwing practice starting position.

131

132

133

132. Practice pivots, pulling on the ends of the rope to simulate an opponent's body resistance.

133. Practice arm maneuvering actions and combine them with leg actions to simulate coordinated arm-body-leg actions which would put you into position to throw.

Using the principle of shadow boxing, you can shadow throw. It will accelerate your development and allow you to practice the preliminary actions with as many repetitions as you need. Moving in for a throw with speed, grace and technical precision is a most important part of judo skill. If you do not move into position quickly, your opponent will not be there for you to throw. If you move in awkwardly, you will not be in good throwing position.

The photos are in pairs, so that you can study the action as it would be done with a partner and compare it with the solo practice procedure. Practice all throws in solo form.

134, 135. From a standard starting position . . .

136, 137. . . . pivot . . .

138, 139. . . . and balance your shadow opponent . . .

140, 141. . . . and complete the action of the throw . . .

142, 143. . . . taking a strong ending position at the completion
of the throw.

PRACTICE WITHOUT ENDINGS

In addition to the many techniques which can be improved through solo practice, there are techniques which can be practiced with a partner who cannot be thrown. If your partner is not skilled in falling techniques, or if there is no mat or other suitable surface available for practice, or if you simply wish to concentrate on the essential preliminary movements, you can practice by taking your partner to the point at which the throw is inevitable, and then return to the starting position.

144-146. As is clear in the photos, tori has completed the actions which are essential to a successful throw. From the position in photo 146, the throw is inevitable. You can practice many of the throwing techniques to off balance.

144

145

146

147

148

HOW TO BLOCK THROWS

With experience, judo players become so sensitive to a throwing attempt that they quickly respond with the appropriate shift of weight or body movement which nullifies the attempt.

In judo contest between players who are relatively inexperienced, there is characteristically a great deal of action: many throws are attempted, there are flurries of perceivable blocks and counter-throwing attempts, and a relatively high proportion of throws are completed.

High-level contests are characterized by relatively few completed throws; good players are less vulnerable to setups and are quick to shift and block.

Here are some examples.

147. The left player has moved into position to attempt a body throw which the right player blocks by pushing at his opponent's lower back or hip. The right player's action shifts his opponent's weight and puts him in awkward position.

148. Or if the right player reacts quickly, he can take a step back, maintaining his hand grips to pull his opponent into backward off-balance.

149. As the body throw is attempted, the right player uses arm action to push his opponent to the left, off balance.

150. As the right player attempts a throw, the left player extends his arms to push his opponent off balance.

151. As the left player attempts a leg throw, the right player pushes the leg with his hand.

149

150

151

152

152. As the left player attempts a circle throw, the right player squats low and shifts his weight back.

In none of these instances does the blocking action involve a struggle or the use of strength. Skillful blocking can be a slight movement or slight shift of weight or position. A skillful player can lightly step over the leg of an opponent to evade a leg throw, or step back to avoid a leg throw.

As you gain experience, you will sense the subtle clues which indicate that your opponent is trying to set you up for a throw. Quick responses to attempted set-up and the ability to use the opponent's attempt to one's own advantage indicate a high level of contest judo proficiency.

153

154

COMBINATION THROWS

Combination throws are used in two ways. If you attempt a
throw which is blocked or unsuccessful, you should be prepared
to move into position for a different throw. The other application of combinations involves a feinting or faking tactic; you
simulate an attempt to throw in order to put your opponent
player in position for a different throw. The first use is by
chance--you apply whatever throw is possible if the first throw
does not succeed. The second use of the combination is
deliberate--your followup throw is planned. Examples of both
uses of combination throws follow.

SWEEPING-FOOT/STRAIGHT-LEG THROW

153. Tori attempts a sweeping-foot throw, which uke opposes
by pulling back.

154. Going with the pulling action of his opponent, tori pivots
on his left foot and swings his right leg into position to apply
the straight-leg throw.

SWEEPING-FOOT/KICKBACK THROW

In the next example, the right player attempts a throw and when
he is blocked, moves in for a second attempt.

155. A sweeping-foot throw, attempted by the right player, is
blocked . . .

156. . . . when the left player braces his right foot onto the mat
and shifts his weight back. The right player, taking advantage of
his opponent's backward shift, steps in to apply a kickback
throw.

155 **156**

157 **158**

SWEEPING-FOOT/UPPER INNERCUT THROW

157. Tori attempts a sweeping-foot throw . . .

158. . . . and then pivots on his left foot, into position for the upper innercut throw. He has chosen the upper innercut because uke's legs are spread.

159   160

161

STRAIGHT-LEG/UPPER INNERCUT THROW

159. Tori attempts a straight-leg throw, and . . .

160. . . . uke steps over the straight leg to evade the throwing attempt . . .

161. . . . and without any change in position, the upper inner-cut throw can be applied.

This is an excellent combination because the transition can be made quickly without a pivot or a shift of balance.

162

163

164

STRAIGHT-LEG/KICKBACK THROW

162. Tori's attempted straight-leg throw is blocked--uke bends tori's knee with his knee. As he blocks the knee, uke pulls back.

163. Going with uke's movement, tori pivots on the ball of his right foot and steps around with the left foot as he pushes uke in the direction he is pulling . . .

164. . . . and applies a kickback throw.

| 165 | 166 |

LEG BLOCK/LATERAL SACRIFICE THROW

165. Tori feints with a leg block which is opposed by uke who shifts his weight in the opposite direction.

166. Going with his opponent's movement, tori places his left foot down so that he faces uke's side, in position to execute a lateral sacrifice throw . . .

167. . . . quickly placing his right foot at uke's left leg and beginning the arm wheeling action in the direction in which uke is moving . . .

168. . . . continuing the arm wheel and sitting down to complete the throw.

167

168

169

170

LIFTING SWEEPING-FOOT/OUTERCUT THROW

169. Tori attempts a lifting sweeping-foot throw which uke resists by pulling back.

170. Going with his opponent's backward movement, tori executes an outercut throw.

171

172

BACK SWEEPING-FOOT/KICKBACK THROW

171. After attempting an unsuccessful back sweeping-foot throw . . .

172. . . . tori steps in for a kickback throw.

173

INSIDE SWEEPING-FOOT/PULLING-DOWN STRAIGHT-LEG THROW

173. Tori feints with an inside sweeping-foot throw . . .

174. . . . and without putting his right foot onto the mat, pivots on the ball of his left foot, swinging himself around . . .

175. . . . and drops into position for a pulling-down straight-leg throw.

174

175

176

177

SWEEPING-FOOT/SWEEPING-THIGH THROW

176. Tori feints a sweeping-foot throw . . .

177. . . . and without putting his right foot on the mat, he pivots on the ball of his left foot and applies a sweeping-thigh throw.

178

179

SPRING-LEG/OUTERCUT THROW

178. A spring-leg throw is attempted by tori, which uke opposes by shifting his weight back . . .

179. . . . making him vulnerable to the outercut throw. Note that tori has put his right foot down and moved clockwise, going with his opponent's movement.

180

181

CIRCLE/INSIDE LATERAL SACRIFICE THROW

180. Tori attempts a circle throw, which his opponent blocks by squatting . . .

181. . . . and tori responds by applying an inside lateral sacrifice throw.

182   183

BINDING/PULLING-DOWN STRAIGHT-LEG THROW

182. Tori feints with a binding throw . . .

183. . . . then drops into position for a pulling-down straight-leg throw.

184   185

SPRING-LEG/OUTERCUT THROW

184. Tori attempts a spring-leg throw, to which his opponent responds by shifting his weight back . . .

185. . . . putting him into vulnerable position for the outercut, throw. Without putting his right foot on the mat, tori applies an outercut throw with his bent right leg.

FALLS — UKEMI

The fear of falling is one of the few instincts exhibited by human babies. The fear of falling persists through life unless training and practice modify the fear or overcome it altogether.

The automatic, untrained response to falling is not safe. Although we do, almost automatically, protect our heads, we expose the other vulnerable body points to the full impact of a fall. Putting a hand out to catch oneself is likely to result in injury; the major impact is concentrated onto the vulnerable wrist. Stiffening up is likely to result in injury because of the crashing impact the body makes when it is rigid.

Falling in a way which spreads impact force over a great surface and reduces the danger of trauma, has to be taught and practiced as it is in judo, wrestling and dancing. No judo player can achieve excellence by learning only the throwing techniques; he must learn to throw and be thrown with equal facility. Then he can achieve the relaxed, easy style which characterizes the best judo play. Even a slight aversion to being thrown can interfere with good judo style. The best player is one who can move easily back and forth from tactics of defense and offense in contest. Aversion to being thrown results in purely defensive tactics and limits a player's development.

Develop and maintain skill in falling techniques for your personal safety and for flexibility in your style.

Judo falls are, in themselves, an excellent form of warmup exercise. They are splendid to learn for accident prevention in daily life. Once you have learned and practiced the safety falls of judo, you should be considerably less liable to injury if you slip or fall accidentally.

BASIC BACK FALL

This is a practice procedure preliminary to learning how to fall from a standing position. The principle of safe falling is demonstrated in this first fall: Avoid jarring impact onto your head, elbows and wrists.

186. Begin from a seated position, your hands at your knees, with your back slightly rounded and your head slightly forward.

187. Keeping your back curled, fall back gently with a rolling (not a thrusting) action as you raise your arms and legs. Your hands are slightly cupped, palms down, fingers spread.

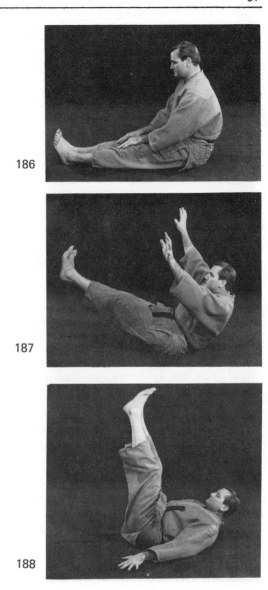

186

187

188

188. As your lower back touches the mat, you slap vigorously
with both hands. The slapping action absorbs impact shock if
the timing is correct. If you slap too soon or too late, the slap
does not function. Avoid hitting the mat with your wrists bent.
Avoid hitting the mat with your arms bent. Your arms are
fully extended as you slap so that your hands and forearms hit
the mat. The larger the hitting surface, the more impact is
absorbed. Your head does not touch the mat.

At the completion of the fall your legs are raised and your fully extended arms are somewhat away from your body. Study the photo to learn the correct ending position.

There are two distinct actions in this fall--one is relaxed and gentle and one is vigorous and forceful. The forceful slapping action is the focus of intensity. The gentle rolling back action is an easy, relaxed movement. The object of much of judo practice is to learn how to concentrate energy in one body movement while avoiding tension and rigidity in the rest of your body.

Practice the two separate kinds of movement, one at a time.

First, lie down full length on the mat, without allowing your head to touch the mat. Keeping your body as relaxed as possible, raise your fully extended arms and slap the mat as hard as you can with your slightly cupped palms. Your arms should be hitting the mat at the angle shown. If you hit the mat in too close to your body, or too far away, it is not efficient. Your fingers should be slightly spread.

Then, start from a seated position, with your head bent slightly forward and your back somewhat curled. As you raise your legs, fall back very gently in a rolling, relaxed manner, without letting your head touch the mat. Avoid stiffness or rigidity.

After you have practiced the slapping and rolling actions, combine them. Concentrate on maintaining ease in your rolling body movement while increasing the vigor of your slapping action.

BASIC SIDE FALL

A combination of gentle, rolling body action and vigorous hand and foot slaps is essential in this practice procedure. New students may have some difficulty coordinating the use of opposite hand and foot, but with practice it can be done effortlessly.

189. Begin supine on the mat, with your head raised. Your head does not touch the mat throughout this procedure. You will roll to your left side first. Raise your left hand and arm, as shown, palm up, in preparation for slapping the mat. Before you begin the physical action, *think* about what you are going to do next. You are going to roll onto your left side and slap the mat with your left hand; as you roll over, you will throw your right leg over your body and hit the mat with the bottom of your right foot.

189

190

190. Rolling easily onto your left side, slap the mat with the palm of your slightly cupped left hand and with the bottom of your right foot. The hand and foot hit the mat at the same time. Your arm is fully extended (not bent) and is not too close to your body. Your fingers are slightly spread. Your head is off the mat. Your right arm is raised in preparation for rolling to your right side. Your body is relaxed, but your hand and foot slaps are vigorous.

The exact angle of your arm is determined with practice. You can feel the correct arm position by the degree of impact which is absorbed by the slap. Your knee is bent enough to permit the full surface of the bottom of your foot to make contact with the mat. Avoid hitting with your toes or the ball of your foot only.

Practice this falling procedure from side to side, slowly at first, without hesitation. Concentrate on coordination of opposite hand and foot movement and upon relaxed rolling body movement.

With practice, hand and foot slapping actions will become more and more vigorous while body movement will become increasingly more relaxed.

My preference is for the ending as shown in photo 190. The groin is well protected by the crossed leg. If tori should lose his balance and fall onto uke, the crossed leg prevents pain or injury to the groin or abdomen. With the leg crossed and the foot braced onto the mat, uke is in a good position to defend against mat work. The crossed-leg ending reduces the possibility of uke landing on his tail bone.

191

192

193

191. The variation shown here is technically correct and is preferred by some.

192. Another variation, shown here, is technically correct, although in my view it lacks the safety factors of the crossed-over leg ending.

193. This ending is appropriate if your feet are swept high as in the application of the side sweeping-foot throw.

194

195

196

STANDING BACK FALL

Start from a relaxed standing position, with your arms extended forward.

194. Bend down as though to touch your toes as you shift your weight onto your right foot . . .

195. . . . and extend your left leg and sit down as close as possible to your right heel, raising your arms as you lower your body . . .

196. . . . rolling backward gently. Slap the mat with both hands just as your lower back touches the mat. Raise your legs as you fall.

In the ending position, your head is off the mat and your arms are fully extended. Avoid thrusting yourself back. Your slapping action should be vigorous. If you lower your body as much as possible before you roll back, you will be able to roll with the least impact onto your back.

197

198

199

200

WALKING SIDE FALL

197. Start from a standing position. To practice falling on your left side, extend your right leg and arm forward, swing your left arm back, as shown . . .

198. . . . and take three gliding steps forward, keeping your right arm and leg advanced and swinging your left arm upward with each step. At the third step, raise your left arm and your left leg, both fully extended . . .

199. . . . and lower your body by bending your right leg and sitting down--do not *thrust* yourself down. This is an easy, relaxed action. As you lower your body, turn onto your left side and when your left buttock barely touches the mat, slap vigorously with your left hand, rolling back without hesitation . . .

200. . . . to finish in this ending position with both legs raised, your head well off the mat.

Avoid catching yourself with your elbow or wrist. Your open hand and arm take most of the impact. Your rolling action prevents full impact on your left hip. The dual actions are a gentle, non-rigid, rolling body movement and a vigorous slap.

ROLLING OVER

Some people experience disorientation when doing a somersault. There will also be a tensing or tightening of the body, which is an impediment to learning the rolling falls. Most people can overcome the sensation of disorientation with moderate practice of simple somersaults. If you are quite comfortable about rolling over or somersaulting, you may omit this procedure.

201. Kneel on the mat with your back curled and your hands palm down, as shown.

202. Place your head lightly on the mat and gently roll over on your back . . .

203. . . . straightening your legs as you go over . . .

204. . . . and end in the seated position shown.

201

202

203

204

205   206

Repeat the procedure until you feel relaxed when you roll over.

205. Then start the rolling action from a standing position . . .

206. . . . pushing yourself over gently with the balls of your feet.

When you can roll over comfortably, proceed to the rolling falls.

207   208

FORWARD ROLL

207. Start with your feet about shoulder width apart, squatting down close to the mat, as shown. Your hands are placed in front of your feet with your fingers pointed out to the sides.

208. Tuck your head in, shift your weight onto your hands and roll over smoothly . . .

209

209. . . . bending your knees as your legs go over so that you finish with a simultaneous slapping action with both hands and both feet.

Study the ending position. Your hips do not hit the mat at all. Your head is off the mat. Your knees are bent. The impact of the fall is spread over your extended arms and the bottoms of both feet.

210

211

STANDING FORWARD ROLL

Start from a relaxed standing position with your arms folded over your head.

210. Lower yourself to the mat as you lean forward and . . .

211. . . . push yourself with enough force to start rolling over and to . . .

212

212. . . . give you enough momentum to continue the rolling
action until you are on your feet in the beginning standing
position.

If you thrust your arms forward as you start to come up, it will
help you rise. If you have difficulty with this procedure, begin
from a spread-legged standing position.

ROLLING SIDE FALL

This practice procedure takes you a step further toward the
practice of falling correctly when thrown. In this practice, you
combine the elements of rolling over smoothly and gently, and
slapping vigorously with opposite hand and foot.

Before you begin the fall, think of an imaginary line which
begins at your left hand, extends along your left arm, over your
left shoulder and across your back to end at your right hip. This
will be the line of your fall. A clear mental image of the line of
fall will help you practice.

213. Begin with your feet placed on a straight line, spread somewhat further apart than shoulder width. Bend your knees and
place your right hand on the mat in front of you (to form a
triangle with your feet), and place your left hand down on the
mat under your head, with your fingers pointed toward your
right foot. Your left elbow points away from your body at a
45-degree angle. Study the photo to see the correct beginning
position clearly. Now concentrate on the idea that your roll
should be smooth and gentle and that your slapping actions will
be vigorous and lively.

214. As you tuck your head in, shift your weight onto your left hand and left foot, raising your right leg and beginning a slow, gentle roll along your left arm . . .

215. . . . over your left shoulder . . .

216. . . . across your back, positioning your right hand to slap the mat . . . and crossing your left leg as you complete the rolling action onto your right side, slapping with your right hand and the bottom of your left foot. The ending position is exactly the same as for the basic side fall.

Check your ending position. Your slapping hand should not be too close or too far out from your body. Your foot should be flat on the mat. Your head is off the mat.

Practice rolling over your right side to end on your left side, slapping with your left hand and the bottom of your right foot.

Avoid going straight over your head. Avoid thrusting your body over. Practice to achieve a rolling action. If you bump your head or jar your shoulder as you go over, you are not working correctly. Slow motion practice is the best way to correct mistakes of technique. When you can do the fall correctly, without any sensation of jarring, practice a faster roll.

In randori there are more throws which put you onto your left side than onto your right side, but you should develop the ability to receive right or left side throws with equal skill.

217

218

SIDE ROLL TO STANDING

The essential movement of this fall is exactly the same as for the previous fall. Instead of beginning from a crouching position, you will begin from a standing stance. Continuity of action is necessary to complete the roll and come back up on your feet.

217. Place your hands out in front of you, as shown, to make certain that you put them down onto the mat in the correct position. Take a step with your left foot and lead with your left elbow . . .

218. . . . bending your right leg as you lower yourself to the mat and shift your weight onto your hands, and without hesitation start the forward roll, using your bent right leg to give you forward momentum, slapping the mat vigorously with your hand and then thrusting with your right hand to help the . . .

219   220

219. . . . continuing forward movement . . .

220. . . . to a standing position, pivoting to face in the direction of your starting position to simulate facing the opponent player.

221

LEAPING ROLL

221. When you can perform the preceding rolling fall comfortably and smoothly, begin practicing the same fall over a small object. Using a duffel bag filled with crumpled paper, take a few steps and a little leap over the bag, completing the fall in a standing position, facing your starting point. You may place your hands on the mat as you roll, or you may make fists of your hands and place the sides of your fists on the mat as you go over. When you can do the fall over a small object, increase the height of the object until you develop the ability to leap higher and higher. Practice the leaping roll over your left and over your right side.

222

223

224

225

FORWARD FALL

222. The beginner's starting position for this fall is on your knees with your hands raised, as shown.

223. Fall forward easily, slapping the mat with both hands slightly cupped, fingers spread. Your ending position is with your weight completely onto your hands and forearms. Your hands and forearms are straight. Avoid bending your wrists or you will feel jarring impact at the wrist joints.

224, 225. When you have practiced this version of the fall so that you absorb impact correctly, you may proceed to the standing version of the fall. From a relaxed standing position, fall forward easily, keeping your body fairly straight and making contact with the mat along your forearms and hands. The rest of your body does not hit the mat. Study the photo to observe the correct ending position. You must *not* hit the mat with bent wrists.

ADVANCED FALLS

If a judo club or group is practicing the advanced falls without a highly experienced teacher, it would be prudent to ask for advice and assistance from a tumbling coach. The procedures and training methods for learning tumbling and stemies are similar.

226

227

228

229

LEAPING BACK FALL

226-229.   From a standing position, squat and swing your arms up as you spring up from the balls of your feet and thrust your hips and legs up, falling onto your back with your legs raised, slapping the mat with your extended arms and the palms of your slightly cupped hands. Your head is off the mat.

230

231

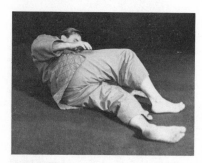

232

LEAPING ROLL

230. From a walking start, leading with your right foot, swing your right arm high and then thrust it down as you ...

231. ... tuck your head in, spring up from your right foot and twist over ...

232. ... to finish on your side. Your extended arm and hand and the bottom of your right foot slap the mat to absorb impact. Your head does not touch the mat.

LEAPING ROLL TO STANDING

Practice the leaping roll, but continue moving--pushing with your slapping hand and foot to assist you in rising to a standing position.

233

234

235

236

LEAPING FORWARD FLIP

233. From a walking or running start, fling your arms back . . .

234. . . . and leap up from one foot as you . . .

235. . . . fling your body over in a flying somersault . . .

236. . . . to finish on your upper back, slapping with both hands and with the bottoms of your feet to absorb impact. Your head and hips do not touch the mat.

237

238

239

LEAPING SIDE FALL

237. From a walking start, fling your arm and leg up vigorously . . .

238. . . . as you leap up and turn your body to the side on which you will fall . . .

239. . . . ending as shown.

FORWARD LEAP

240. From a walking start, or from a standstill, crouch slightly as you fling your arms back . . .

241. . . . leaping up from the balls of your feet. Straighten your legs in the air . . .

242. . . . and fall forward onto your forearms. The balls of your feet hit the mat and you absorb impact along your forearms and hands. Your face is well off the mat. Your wrists must not be bent. The line from your elbow to your fingertips is perfectly straight.

243

SIDE SHOULDER HOLD – BASIC HOLD

243. Sit in tight and close to your partner's right side. Put your right arm around his neck, placing your right palm on the mat. Your left hand grips cloth at his upper arm and you lock his right arm under your left arm. Your right knee is wedged into his right shoulder. Your left leg is extended and the bottom of your left foot is braced onto the mat. As an additional brace, you can lock your head tightly into his body, as in photo 244.

244

SIDE SHOULDER HOLD – FIRST VARIATION

244. From the basic hold, your partner frees his right arm. Pin his right arm with your left leg. Though you are not as well braced with your left leg in this position, you can apply pressure on the pinned arm with your leg, inhibiting his movement.

245

SIDE SHOULDER HOLD — SECOND VARIATION

245. From the basic hold, your partner frees his right arm and holds it up. With your left hand, push his right arm across his neck and lock it between your head and shoulder. Regrip cloth at his shoulder with your left hand.

246

SIDE SHOULDER HOLD — THIRD VARIATION

246. Your partner hooks your leg with his leg, pulling your upper body back. As you are pulled back, slide your left arm over and around his right leg and grab your own pant legs high at the thighs, both hands gripping cloth. To apply pressure, press inward with your arms and straighten your legs. Release immediately when he taps.

247

248

249

SIDE SHOULDER HOLD — FIRST ESCAPE

You are captured in a side shoulder hold.

247. Push at your opponent's knee with your right hand.

248. Hook his knee with your left foot.

249. Use your entire body to roll toward your left. As you pull his leg with your leg, grab cloth at his left shoulder with your left hand and pull sharply, and with your right hand grip cloth at his chest and push. All these actions must be coordinated to effect escape.

250

251

SIDE SHOULDER HOLD — SECOND ESCAPE

250. Fling your body and legs to the left and then . . .

251. . . . reverse the action, flinging your body and legs to the right, twisting your body as you turn and drawing your right arm under you. This action might have to be repeated several times to effect escape.

252

SIDE SHOULDER HOLD — THIRD ESCAPE

252. With both hands, grip his belt at the back and bridge your body upward as you jerk up on his belt, getting his hip off the mat, and . . .

253   254

253. . . . when his hip is off the mat, slide your right knee under his hip.

254. Effect escape by rolling to the left as you raise him with your knee and pull him over you with both arms.

255

CROSS-BODY HOLD — BASIC HOLD

255. Working from the right side of your partner, your body is across his upper body; your left knee is wedged into his armpit; your right knee is wedged into his side, just above his hip. Your left elbow is locked into the left side of his neck; your right elbow is locked into his left side just above the hip bone. Grip cloth with both hands. Keep your head down.

256

CROSS-BODY HOLD — FIRST VARIATION

256. Your partner simulates an attempted escape, using his left arm to work himself free. Grip his wrist with your right hand. With your left hand, reach under his arm and grip your own right wrist with your left hand. Locking pressure is applied by forcing down with your right hand as you lever up with your left arm.

257

CROSS-BODY HOLD — SECOND VARIATION

257. From the basic hold, your partner attempts to roll you over and off. To establish a counterweight, you straighten both legs and shift your weight onto your elbows, the balls of your feet and onto his chest.

258

CROSS-BODY HOLD — THIRD VARIATION

258. From the basic hold, your partner attempts to slide out from under. Reach under his head with your left arm and grip cloth at your own pant leg at the thigh. Cinch your elbows and knees tightly into his sides. If he moves, tighten your locking action.

259

260

261

CROSS-BODY HOLD — FIRST ESCAPE

259. You are pinned in a cross-body hold.

260. Grip the back of his jacket with your left hand. Grip his belt with your right hand. At the same time, brace your feet and push him toward your right side with your body and arms.

261. His reaction to your pushing action will be to oppose it. Going with his opposing movement, reverse your action and pull him over you with your arms, rolling your body to help you effect release.

262   263

CROSS-BODY HOLD — SECOND ESCAPE

262. With your left hand grip the back of his jacket and pull him toward your left, using body motion to assist the pull. With your right hand push his left foot, reducing some of his bracing strength.

263. His reaction will be to oppose your action by pulling back. Going with his reaction, jerk your body to the right as you push with your left hand. With your right hand, keep his left leg locked. Your braced leg will help you bridge your body as you twist to the right.

CROSS-BODY HOLD — THIRD ESCAPE

264. Grip his belt at the back with your right hand and grip cloth at his lapel with your left. Using both hands, push him toward your feet. He resists and you go with his action, pulling back sharply and using body motion to roll him over.

264

265

TOP-BODY HOLD

265. Place your body lengthwise over your partner's body with your head pressed into his body just above the belt. Your legs are drawn up, with weight on your knees and elbows. With both hands grip his belt at his sides and lock your elbows into his shoulders.

266

TOP-BODY HOLD — FIRST VARIATION

266. This is like the basic hold, except that his arms are not pinned with your arms. Your elbows are locked into his sides.

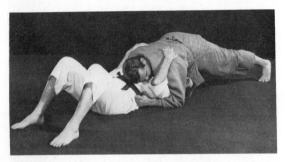

267

TOP-BODY HOLD — SECOND VARIATION

267. From the basic hold, extend your legs and brace your toes onto the mat, spreading your legs to form a tripod with your upper body.

268

TOP-BODY HOLD — THIRD VARIATION

268. With his left hand he is attempting to pull you off. Slide your left hand under his upper arm and over his wrist. Pressure can be applied by pulling back with your left hand.

269

270

271

TOP-BODY HOLD — FIRST ESCAPE

269. You are pinned in a top-body hold.

270. With both hands, grip his belt at the back as you swing your legs in a whipping action to the right side.

271. As he resists your action, go with his reaction--whip your legs over toward the left as you twist him with your arms, and . . .

272. . . . effect release, and . . .

273. . . . apply a top-body hold on him.

274

275

TOP-BODY HOLD — SECOND ESCAPE

274. Bracing your feet on the mat with your knees bent as shown, arch your body upward as you pull up with both hands gripping the back of his belt.

275. Thrust him backward with your hands as you drop down and slide forward.

276

277

TOP-BODY HOLD — THIRD ESCAPE

276. Swing your legs over sharply and place them at a 90-degree angle to his body, as you pull up with both your hands at the back of his belt.

277. Repeat the swinging leg movement once or twice and complete the escape by rolling over onto your side.

278

STRADDLING-BODY HOLD

278. Kneeling, braced on your toes, your knees are at his hips. Your arms are under his arms, gripping cloth at his shoulders. Your chest is on his chest; your head is placed next to his head. The hold is maintained by pulling toward you with your arms and squeezing in with your knees.

To escape from this hold, use the techniques for release from the top-body hold.

279

280

REVERSE SIDE-SHOULDER HOLD

279. Sitting on your right hip, lock your right knee firmly into uke's side. The bottom of your left foot is braced onto the mat, but moveable if he tries to escape. Your right arm is under his neck and grasps cloth at his shoulder. Your left hand grips his belt at his right side. Maintain the hold by wedging him into your right leg with your arms. Press your upper body onto his chest to prevent escape.

280. The same hold from a different view.

To effect release, use the techniques for escape from the cross-body hold.

ARM-AND-HEAD SHOULDER HOLD

281. Sitting on your right hip, your right leg is wedged under uke's right shoulder. Your left foot is braced on the mat. The upper part of your body lies across his chest. Your right arm is locked into his left side. Your right hand grips cloth at his left shoulder. Your left arm is locked at the left side of his head and grips cloth under his left shoulder. Keep your head down, squeeze your body into his chest, and lock him between your right leg and your arms.

282. The same hold, different view.

To effect release, use the techniques for escape from the side-body hold.

281

282

283

KNEELING SIDE-SHOULDER HOLD

283. Kneeling on your right knee, place it at uke's right side.
Your left leg is extended with your foot braced on the mat.
Your right arm is around his neck, gripping cloth at his right
shoulder. Your head and shoulder are braced into his head,
neck and shoulder. Your left hand grips cloth at his right upper
arm. Maintain the hold by clamping him between your right
arm and right knee, with your left foot acting as a brace.

To effect release, use the techniques for release from the side-
body hold.

CHANGING MAT HOLDS

When you have applied a mat hold from which your opponent is attempting escape, you have the option of moving to a variation, or you can change to a different hold. Mat work practice should include both forms of responding to an escape attempt.

Your partner will offer only token resistance until you have learned the fundamentals of changing from hold to hold.

Two examples are shown.

284. Start with a side shoulder hold.

285, 286. As your partner begins to escape, change to a cross-body hold and . . .

287, 288. . . . as he begins to escape from the cross-body hold, change to a top-body hold.

You should practice this type of action changing from hold to hold as the escape is simulated.

The move from one hold to the next should be done without hesitation.

284

285

286

287

288

289

290

291

292

CHANGING MAT HOLDS —

SOLO PRACTICE

289-292. To practice the basic body movements of quick change from mat hold to mat hold, you can work alone. Using an imaginary opponent, change your position to simulate going from hold to hold.

293

BENT-ARM LOCK — IN

293. Uke is on his back. You are seated at his left side with
your left elbow locked into his side. With your left hand you
grip his left wrist with an unnatural grip. Slide your right hand
under his captured arm and grip your own left wrist. The lock
is maintained by cinching his captured arm tightly into your
body as you lean into his arm.

STRAIGHT-ARM LOCK — OUT WITH ARM PRESSURE

294. Uke is on his back. You are seated at his left side. Grip
his left wrist with your right hand. Reach under his left arm
at the elbow and grip your own right wrist. Pressure is applied
by levering down on his wrist with your right hand, leaning
back into his body and pushing up at his elbow with your left
forearm.

STRAIGHT-ARM LOCK — UP WITH LEG PRESSURE

295. Uke is lying face down with his right arm extended.
Kneel at his right side on your right knee, with your left leg
over his extended arm. Grip his right wrist with both your
hands, keeping the captured arm extended, palm up. Your
left thigh should be positioned at his elbow, your left leg is
fully extended and your foot is braced into the mat. Pressure
is applied by levering up on his captured arm.

STRAIGHT-ARM LOCK WITH HIP PRESSURE

296. Uke is on his back and you are lying on your back with
your left leg across his neck; you have captured his right
extended arm with both your hands. Your hip is in close to
his shoulder and the top of your right foot is wedged into his
right side. Pressure is applied by levering his elbow against
either of your thighs as you raise your hips.

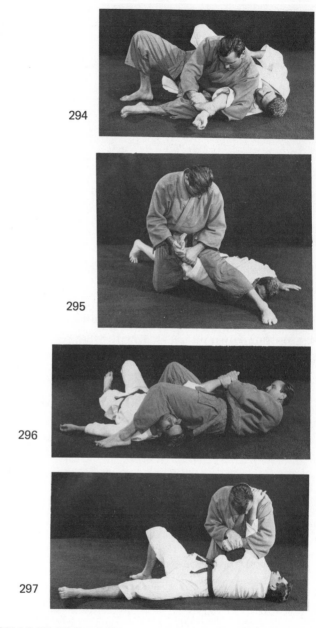

294

295

296

297

STRAIGHT-ARM LOCK INTO BODY

297. Uke is lying on his back, his left arm extended. Kneel at his right side. Lock his left wrist into your neck and shoulder at your left side. Place your left forearm over his left elbow. With your right hand grip your own left hand, and pull into your body.

298

STRAIGHT-ARM LOCK WITH BODY LEVER

298. Uke is face down with his right arm extended. You are seated at his right side with his right arm captured under your left arm and you grip his right wrist with both your hands. Pressure is applied by raising his arm toward his head as you lean in that direction with your upper body.

STRAIGHT-ARM LOCK WITH LEG LEVER

299. Your partner is face down with his right arm extended. You are lying on your right side and you grip his wrist with both hands. Your left leg is crossed over his captured arm at the elbow; your left foot is braced onto the mat; your right leg is wedged into his side. Pressure is applied by raising his captured arm and levering down with your left leg.

COMBINATION STRAIGHT-ARM LOCK/BENT-ARM LOCK

300. Uke is on his back. Lower yourself onto your right knee as you capture his right arm under your left armpit and slide your left arm around the captured arm. Your left forearm is locked under his right elbow; your right hand is placed at his right shoulder. With your left hand grip your own right wrist. Pressure is applied by pushing down at his shoulder with your right hand and raising up against his captured elbow, with your left forearm. Additional leverage can be applied by leaning your upper body back. This lock is effective if uke's arm is extended with the palm up.

301. If uke's arm is bent, the lock is taken in the same manner, but pressure is applied by levering up and *outward* against the captured elbow.

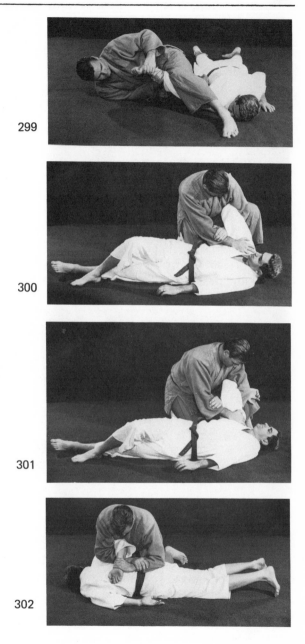

299

300

301

302

REAR BENT-ARM LOCK

302. Uke is face down, with his right arm bent behind his back.
Grip his wrist with your left hand; slide your right hand under
his captured wrist and grip your own left wrist. Pressure is
applied by raising his captured arm toward his head.

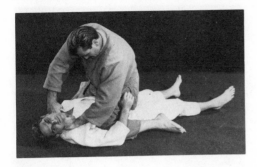

303

KNUCKLE CHOKE

303. With your arms extended, grip cloth at the sides of uke's neck with your fingers inside the jacket, thumbs outside, in an unnatural grip. A slight motion forward will take up the slack. Apply pressure by rotating your fists outward so that your large knuckles press into the *sides* of his neck.

304

305

ONE-ARM CROSS CHOKE

304. You are straddling uke. With your right hand reach across and grip cloth high at his right lapel, using an unnatural grip. With your left hand, grip cloth at his left lapel. Pressure is applied by levering against the *side* of his neck with your right forearm as you pull across with your left arm.

FRONT SLIDING CHOKE

305. With your right hand grip both his lapels in one hand, with your forefinger between the lapels. With your left hand grip his left lapel just below your right hand. Apply pressure by pulling down with your left hand as you slide your right hand up without releasing your grip on the jacket. Pressure is applied by cloth against the *sides* of his neck.

306

CROSSED-ARM CHOKE

306. With crossed hands, grip high at uke's collar with your thumbs inside the cloth, palms down. Pull toward you to take up slack and then apply pressure against the sides of his neck with your forearms. Release pressure *instantly* at the tapping signal.

307   308

LOOP CHOKE

307. Face uke, shown here standing (he could be kneeling), and without crossing your arms, grip cloth at his left lapel with both hands. Pull sharply down and forward . . .

308. . . . and without releasing your hand grips, loop your right arm around his head--an action which will cross your arms. A scissoring action with both arms applies the choke.

REAR FOREARM CHOKE

This choke can be applied only when you are in back of uke.
In tournament, it might be applied if he attempts a throw which
places him in front of you.

309. With your right hand, grip cloth at his left shoulder or
lapel, using a natural grip. Place your left forearm at the right
side of his neck. Apply pressure against the side of his neck
with your forearm as you pull toward you with your right hand.

REAR SLIDING CHOKE

310. First practice this technique from a kneeling position.
It can also be applied if uke is lying supine on the mat. Kneel
behind him. Reach over his left shoulder with your left hand
and grip cloth high at his right collar. With your right hand,
grip cloth at his lapel. Apply pressure by pulling down with
your right hand as you slide your left arm around and back.

UNDER-AND-OVER ARM CHOKE

311. This technique can be applied if uke is lying, kneeling,
or standing. Reach around his neck with your right arm and
grip cloth high at his left shoulder with your right hand; your
forearm must be positioned at the side of his neck, *not at his
windpipe*. Slide your left arm under his left arm, raising his
arm and placing your left hand at the back of his head. Pressure
is applied by pushing with your left hand.

312. A variation of this technique is applied by reaching over
his left arm with your left arm and placing your left fist into
the middle of his back. Pressure is applied by pressing with
your fist.

REAR NECK LOCK CHOKE

313. This technique can be applied if uke is standing, kneeling,
or lying supine. Put your right arm around his neck so that his
windpipe is positioned at the bend of your elbow--this will
avoid putting pressure against the windpipe. Grip your own
left arm with your right hand and put your left hand at the back
of his head. Pressure is applied by pushing forward with your
left hand and tightening the muscles of both arms.

309

310

311

312

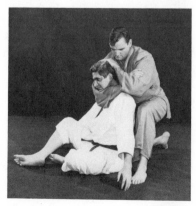

313

RELEASES FROM CHOKES

If a choke has been applied with proper technique, you may not
be able to effect release before the time allowed. If there is any
weakness in the technique, one of the two following escapes
may effect release from a front choke.

A. Press inward at your opponent's elbows with both hands.
This is the weakest area of his arms and relatively little pressure
will effect release.

B. Clasp your hands together between his arms and lever against
his elbows with your forearms.

For your health and safety, tap for release if you feel that a
strong hold has been applied against your neck. If you struggle
to effect release, it may only increase the choking pressure and
that may put you unconscious.

CAUTION: If there is *any* pressure applied against your
windpipe, tap for release! It is dangerous to allow pressure
at this highly vulnerable area.

If you are tori, applying the technique, you must release
the instant you are given the tapping signal. If you have
inadvertently applied pressure to the front of uke's throat
he will not be able to speak.

Whenever you play judo it is essential to observe the
tapping-for-release signal. It is particularly important when
you are practicing the grappling/choking techniques.

RELEASE FROM ARM LOCKS

Arm locks can sometimes be broken in the following manner.
First, grip cloth at your captured arm and oppose the direction
of the push (or pull) to relieve pressure. Then turn your arm
over and bend it. If you are able to turn and bend, you should
be able to escape.

Randori, or free-style practice, is the game of judo. In the same way that the game of chess is based on a knowledge of the possible moves, the game of judo is based upon a knowledge of the basic techniques. But knowing basic techniques is not enough. You are not a chess player if you only know how the pieces move; you must be able to plan a game and follow through with your plan as you cope with the fact that your opponent has a plan which must be prevented from being carried out. Randori is the strategical and tactical use of all possible techniques--offensive and defensive--in appropriate combination. The greater your skill, the more quickly you will be able to act and react. You can develop skill in offensive play; you can develop skill as a defensive player; best, you can develop the skill to plan offensive plays while anticipating and defending against the offensive tactics of the opponent player.

GIVE & TAKE THROWING

Give-and-take throwing practice is an interim procedure which prepares you for randori and for contest.

In give-and-take, each partner throws in turn. Unlike kata formal demonstration, in which the movements are rehearsed and specified, give-and-take players apply any throw which can be executed by plan or by chance. The partners neither resist nor assist the throw. If it is a good attempt, uke will be thrown.

The players grasp each other in the standard manner and move about on the mat, slide-stepping. They use arm and body movement for maneuvering. The player whose turn it is to throw first, throws when he feels that his opponent player is in position for the throw he has planned. Or he throws if his partner puts himself into vulnerable position for a different throw than the one he had planned. Then the players return to the starting position and begin moving about on the mat again, and the other partner throws.

After the basic technique of any throw has been learned, it should be practiced in give-and-take style.

Give-and-take, tactical use of throws and free-style practice are necessary training procedures for players who intend to enter contest, or who wish to have a working knowledge of competitive judo play. Those individuals who are practicing judo solely for the exercise and as recreation and wish to learn only the formal techniques, may eliminate all contest-like training.

INDIVIDUAL STYLE

In judo, as in many other sports, the really great champions
are those with a unique style.

Before you can develop your own style of judo play, you must
first learn the techniques as they are taught by your instructor.
This gives you a point of departure. When you can perform well
in the conventional or traditional style then you can explore the
possibilities of individual development.

The old-style method of teaching judo makes very little allow-
ance for differences in individual style, preference and need.
Modern judo coaches encourage stylistic development to suit
each person.

For tournament, a balanced repertory of techniques would
consist of one or two favored throws, several secondary throws,
the ability to apply *any* throw by chance, and a variety of
matwork techniques. An all-around judo player knows which
techniques are most likely to be successful in contest, and he
develops them to perfection, but he does not neglect the
practice of other throws and matwork which enhance his
general skill.

The judo player who concentrates solely on a limited few
techniques is not an accomplished judoka.

ETIQUETTE

It is a form of courtesy, as well as a rule of safety, for players
to exchange information if they are practicing together for the
first time. If players are not wearing colored belts, or the
color ranking system is unfamiliar, they should tell each other
how long they have been practicing judo and give some indication
of their proficiency level. They should agree beforehand on the
groups of techniques they will use--whether or not, for instance,
they will use mat work or standing chokes.

Judo players who have not previously practiced randori together
should work slowly at first, until they are somewhat familiar with
the style of the opponent player. This would not apply in contest.

SALUTATION BOW

Most competitive sports have a formal salutation. Boxers touch gloves, fencers cross foils, wrestlers shake hands. Judo players bow.

At the beginning of a randori practice session, the players approach each other to a distance of about two meters (approximately six feet), place their hands at their thighs, and bow. Then they rise, take steps toward each other and grasp uniforms in the standard starting position. When they finish the session, they bow to each other before leaving the mat or working out with another player.

The salutation for contest is somewhat more formal and is explained further along.

COURTESY THROW

A formal courtesy is shown by players of lower rank to players of higher rank. When two players of different rank are practicing randori, the lower-degree player allows the higher-degree player to throw first, without opposition. The courtesy throw does not apply in contest or tournament.

KI-AI

Ki-ai, sometimes called ki-ya or ki-yai, is the conscious use of of an energy concentration technique which many of us use without thinking to prepare for a surge of power

You are likely to follow a pattern of behavior, unconsciously, when you have a heavy job to do. First, you take a deep breath which you exhale with a grunt as you complete the action. Ki-ai is the technique of consciously using the inhale and exhale/grunt behavior for focus and concentration.

There are two distinct phases of ki-ai -- the windup and the thrust. The first phase prepares; the second phase delivers.

In the windup phase, concentrate. Take a deep breath, tighten your abdominal muscles, and focus your attention on the action to come. In the thrust phase exhale sharply as you throw.

Ki-ai can be silent (except for the sound of the breath being forcefully expelled) or sounded. When sounded or shouted, different sounds can be used. *Hai* and *ai* are often used, but many judo players shout *zut* or *huh* , or they hiss as they exhale and apply the critical action.

THE GOING-WITH PRINCIPLE

The *going-with* principle in judo is widely misunderstood and misinterpreted. It is usually taken to mean that you simply follow the lead of your opponent. The going-with principle is more complex and encompasses a number of related meanings, among them: Do not oppose force with force. Use the momentum of an action for your own purpose. Find the area of weakness or least resistance to your planned action. Learn to respond flexibly so that you can take advantage of a movement instead of opposing it.

The going-with principle can be applied as a tactic in which you set up your opponent.

For example, you might feint by pushing him as though to put him in weak balance backward. If he responds to the push by pressing forward, you could take advantage of his response and pull him forward and vulnerable to any number of forward-moving throws.

The going-with principle can be applied as a defensive tactic. It can be used as a feinting tactic to give the appearance of being led, and it can be used as a lead into combination throws and counter-throwing.

When your opponent attempts to maneuver you, do not try to oppose his action with force or strength; slide your feet in the direction of his pull or push and then execute a blocking action, an evasive move, or a counter-throw.

BY-CHANCE THROWS AND SET-UP THROWS

Highly skilled judo players must learn to use the set-up throw and must have the ability to throw by chance. Both are important.

By-chance throwing means that you wait for the opportunity to apply a throw when your opponent places himself in a weak or vulnerable balance.

314   315

314, 315. *Setting up* is a deliberate move to put the opponent player in position for your planned throw. You can make him vulnerable by breaking his balance back, or by putting him in weak balance forward. Or, you can use more subtle set-ups as shown in the following pages. If you can improve your skill at set-up throwing, you will gain a distinct advantage in contest.

Of course, you must maintain the ability to throw by chance when a player offers a weak stance and you must be able to apply combination throws when an opportunity presents itself.

SET-UP MANEUVER

316, 317. An example of a set-up throw is shown here. In
photo 316, the right player moves in such a way as to give the
appearance of making an attempt to throw to his right. The
opponent player pulls away, and the right player executes the
planned throw, 317.

Other techniques of setting up for a throw are feints, fakes,
diversions, misleading arm movements, misleading leg and foot
movements--in short, any action which produces a predictable
reaction from your opponent so that you can apply the throw
of your choice.

FALSE OPPORTUNITY SET-UP

Highly skilled players can present themselves in an apparent
weak position, expecting that the other player will respond to
that weakness, attempt a throw--which the skilled player can
block--and follow with a counter-throw.

With practice, you can use this tactic to get exactly the response
you want, and apply your planned throw.

318, 319. This shows the pretense of weakness being offered
by the right player, who puts his foot out as though vulnerable
to a sweeping-foot throw. As the left player attempts the sweep,
the right player pulls his foot away and applies the planned back
hook.

FAKE & THROW

There is a difference between this tactic and the combination
throw. In combinations, you seriously attempt each throw in
your series. In this tactic, you *fake* the first attempt to get
the expected reaction so that you can apply the throw of your
choice. This tactic is a set-up.

320, 321. The right player fakes a throwing attempt, gets the
backward-moving reaction he wants, and then applies the planned
leg throw.

316

317

318

319

320

321

FOLLOW THE LEADER SET-UP

Follow-the-leader is an excellent tactic for putting your opponent off-guard while you get ready for an offensive action. Your strategy is to allow him to take steps which you follow until you can apply your throw. There is a very slight time lag between his movement and yours. It is not a simultaneous action but a deliberate going-in-his direction tactic which gives the impression that you are maneuverable.

322, 323. The left player takes a backward step; the right player follows his lead, ready to throw.

322   323

BY-CHANCE

324. An error is made by the left player. He has allowed himself to be tilted into weak balance; the right player applies a throw in the direction of weakness.

With practice you can become responsive to slight errors, weaknesses and false moves.

324

325   326

HOW TO COPE WITH RETREATING STYLE

A player moving backward constantly protects himself from your throwing attempts and pulls you into vulnerable positions for the application of his throws.

It is easier to apply most throws when your opponent moves toward you rather than away from you.

325, 326. One way to counter the backing-up tactic is to follow along so that he is positioned at the edge of the mat. From this area he must change his direction; when he does, you apply your throw.

327. A second method of dealing with backing up is to move in a circular direction. It is not efficient to resist his backward action by pulling him forward. The circling action interferes with his backward movement without putting you into weak balance. Alternate your circling movements, first to one side and then to the other until he is vulnerable to your throw.

327

328

DEFENSIVE PLAY

An over-emphasis on defensive tactics is common among beginning judo players, especially those whose nervousness about being thrown makes them too cautious in play. A match in which both players are primarily defensive is dull and pointless.

The best judo play is a combination of skill in planning and applying point-winning tactics, and skill in defensive play.

DEFENSIVE STANCE

328. A low crouching stance can be used as a defensive tactic. But when both players assume the low stance and maintain it, it becomes a no-win situation.

Deliberate stalling in contest is poor play and poor sportsmanship. However, there is a way of gaining time in contest under certain conditions which is legal and justified if you have already made a point in a match, you do not feel that you have any chance of making a second point, and your only hope of holding on to your lead is to avoid being thrown.

Shift into a strong, low defensive position from which you would not expect to throw, but which prevents your opponent from throwing. From this position use gliding steps and keep moving, preferably in a circular clockwise direction if your opponent is right-handed, or counterclockwise if your opponent is left-handed.

329

330

IMMEDIATE OFFENSIVE PLAY

329, 330. This tactic works best if you have had a chance to evaluate the opposing player and judge his areas of weakness. It also works well as a surprise tactic if no other player has used it. After bowing, without hesitation, use a leaping pivot and throw.

BELT & CLOTH GRIPS

In contest and in practice, gripping the opponent player's belt continuously is prohibited. It is also prohibited to grip cloth at the leg or at the back of the jacket. But any of the above cloth grips is permitted for the application of a *specific* technique.

A belt grip can be defensive or offensive, or it can be used as a counteraction. A cloth grip can be used to shift an opponent player into weak or off-balance position. When the specific technique has been applied you must regrip in one of the standard ways.

331. As a counteraction to a belt grip by the opponent . player, a return belt grip can be used.

331

332

333

332. As an assist for the application of a throw, the belt can be gripped at the back or side.

333. The belt can be gripped for an upward pull to shift the opponent's weight and balance.

334

334. A cloth grip at the back of the jacket is used here to raise and shift the opponent player into poor balance, vulnerable for a throw.

There are times when you are permitted to grip cloth at your opponent's uniform at the leg--in mat work, for instance, and when it is used as an assist to apply a throw.

335

336

335, 336. A body throw has been attempted and resisted.
Instead of giving up the attempt, you grip cloth low at your
opponent's leg and pull up to shift him into an off-balance
position to assist your throw.

337

338

TIPS FOR TALL MEN

337. A taller player can put a shorter opponent into awkward
balance by gripping the back of his belt and lifting up. With
his balance broken forward, the shorter player is vulnerable
to a throw.

338. Against a shorter opponent who works in a low crouching
position, grip the pant leg and pull up to put him in poor balance.

339   340

339. A tall man can grip his opponent player at the back of the collar and pull up and forward to put his opponent in poor balance.

340. Grip the opponent player's belt at the front and pull up and forward.

All the foregoing tactics must be used skillfully and in conjunction with a good throw. If they are used with force, or if they appear to be rough, or if they seem to interfere with the application of a clean throw, they could invalidate an otherwise point-winning throw.

TIPS FOR SHORT MEN

It is not true that a small man has inherent advantages over a big man in the sport of judo, though that idea was once widely believed. A good judo player has advantages over a poor judo player, regardless of size. Most of the skilled judo players were small men when judo was played almost exclusively by Japanese. Now it is clear that when players have equal skill, there is an advantage in size and height. A shorter player who is highly skilled can take advantage of the size relationship.

341   342

341. If a shorter player keeps his center of gravity low by squatting, a taller player will have difficulty applying a body throw.

342. The shorter man can easily move in for body throws and can learn to use his size as a tactical advantage.

343. Ordinarily, sacrifice throws are more difficult for a shorter man to apply against a taller opponent. But if a taller player moves his upper body forward and maneuvers with his legs backed off (as though to defend against attempted leg throws) he is vulnerable to sacrificing throws.

343

344

MANEUVERING

This training procedure will increase your skill at maneuvering your opponent player in judo contest. No matter how well you can throw, unless you are equally good at setting up for the throw, you must wait for a lucky chance to apply the technique. When you improve your ability to control your opponent's movements, your throwing opportunities will increase considerably.

The object of this practice is to avoid stepping into the square, while trying to maneuver your opponent into it. You are permitted to leap over the area since that indicates you are in control of your own movements. You are not attempting to throw your partner.

Mark a square of about four feet in the center of the mat using chalk or tape. Begin your practice at the edge of the mat.

344, 345. Players work their way around to the corner. The right player uses good arm action to place his opponent into weak balance from which he cannot avoid stepping into the square.

345

346

BLINDFOLDED SPARRING

Working with a severe handicap is an excellent way of improving
judo skill. Observe the safety rules carefully. The partner not
blindfolded must warn you if you get too close to the edge of
the mat. This practice develops sensitivity to subtle movements
and gentle actions which you learn to feel, rather than see. Take
turns being blindfolded. Stop the action when you are in a good
position to throw. The throw need not be applied.

346. Starting from the standard position, the partners practice
free-style, trying a variety of throws.

WEARING SOCKS HANDICAP

Wearing socks for practice is a technique to improve randori
skill. It will be more difficult to maintain your balance. The
way you move, the way you set your weight onto the mat, the
way you respond to your partner's maneuvering will be different
with the handicap of wearing socks.

Blindfolded sparring and sparring wearing socks are difficult
procedures; they are not meant for beginners.

347

348

HALF-POINT THROWS

When a throwing attempt has been effectively blocked and cannot be applied as planned, you can sometimes try for a half point. Ordinarily, officials will not award a full point for a throw in which body weight is used to pull or drag uke down.

347, 348. A leg throw is attempted, unsuccessfully. By dropping down onto the mat, the right player applies body weight to pull his opponent into off-balance and throws. This will sometimes be judged a good, crisp throw for a full point.

349

350

349, 350. A back sweeping-foot throw is attempted, but the timing is off. By sitting down onto the mat, body weight pulls the opponent down into a half-point throw.

351, 352. A body throw is attempted unsuccessfully. By dropping down onto the mat, body weight and arm work take the opponent over for a half-point throw.

COUNTERS AGAINST STIFF-ARMING

Stiff-arming is the procedure of extending the arms rigidly to prevent being thrown. If it is used occasionally, stiff-arming is a good defensive tactic. When a player stiff-arms, he may succeed in preventing a throw, but he is not in a good position to attempt throws. Avoid dependence on stiff-arming. Learn the counters against it.

353. The left player is shown stiff-arming.

354. You can take advantage of his forward pushing movement to apply a lifting sweeping-foot throw.

355

356

355. In response to the left player's stiff-arming tactic, the right player uses his forearm to bend the elbow . . .

356. . . . and takes advantage of his opponent's awkward balance to apply a throw.

Hitting is illegal. You may not apply a blow to bend his stiff arm. The action shown in photo 355 is a levering, pressing action.

357

358

357. The left player is stiff-arming. The right player releases his left hand grip on his opponent's jacket . . .

358. . . . and regrips cloth at his shoulder, pulling to tilt his opponent off balance . . .

359. . . . and applies a leg throw.

360

360. As the left player stiff-arms, the right player pushes up under his opponent's arms and moves in . . .

361. . . . for the throw.

362

362. Taking advantage of the opponent player's stiff-arming tactic, the right player pulls him forward and applies a sacrificing throw.

363   364

363. As the left player stiff-arms, the right player grips his opponent's belt and pulls him forward sharply . . .

364. . . . and applies the throw.

365   366

365. As the left player stiff-arms, the right player grips cloth at the back of the collar and pulls his opponent forward . . .

366. . . . for the throw.

The rules of judo prohibit any action which could be interpreted as applying force in the execution of a throw. Grasping the opponent player's belt or cloth at his shoulder or the back of his collar would only be permitted if those actions preceded and flowed into a crisp and technically correct throw. If it appeared that the force of the grabbing action *dragged* the opponent down, it would invalidate the throw.

MAT WORK TACTICS

In contest, you can earn points for throwing and for mat work. If a throw is attempted and is not point-winning, you could be in a position to apply a mat work technique to gain a point. Or you could apply a successful, point-winning throw and earn an additional point for mat work. You must make a clean throw before attempting the mat work. If you follow uke onto the mat too quickly it might appear that you had lost your balance in the process of throwing, which would invalidate the throwing point. On the other hand, if you hesitate too long, uke might recover and protect himself from follow-up mat work. There are some mat work techniques which can be started as uke is falling.

Other instances in which you could apply mat work are: The opponent player goes onto the mat accidentally. The opponent player attempts a sacrificing throw but does not succeed and he is in position for your mat work. The opponent player applies a successful sacrificing throw but does not protect himself from your mat work attempt.

ADDING POINTS WITH MAT WORK

A good player can apply throws successfully in contest for the full point. A superior player can apply the throw and move swiftly in for mat work to insure or increase the score.

He can either gain a full additional point for good mat work, or salvage a half-point throw by the use of tactics on the ground.

If you are to earn points for throwing *and* for mat work, your throw must be a good, clean throw. If the officials see what might be interpreted as a stumbling down onto the mat, they might award a point for mat work but not for the throw.

To demonstrate the crispness of a good, planned throw, timing is important. If you hesitate for a fraction of a second after you throw, you demonstrate full control; if you hesitate too long, you will lose the opportunity for ground work.

367

368

367, 368. The series shows perfect timing. The first shows the completeness of the throw, with the thrower still well-balanced and in control; he moves down onto the mat before his opponent player can recover; he applies the mat hold firmly.

369

DEFENSIVE TACTICS TO PREVENT MAT WORK

369. You have been thrown. Before your opponent can apply ground work, draw your knees up toward your head and guard your head with your arms.

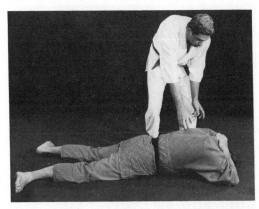

370

370. You have been thrown. Roll over and spread your legs, brace yourself into the mat, grip the back of your collar with both hands.

371

372

371, 372. After being thrown, roll away from your opponent, rolling over several times before you rise.

373

374

THROW & LEAP

When working with a player who tends to try to drag his
opponent down if he is thrown, be prepared to save your full
point by leaping or stepping into a strong, balanced ending
stance. This will show the judges that you have executed a
crisp, full-point throw. Otherwise, you are in danger of being
pulled into awkward balance and losing half of a point.

373, 374. As the throw is completed but before your opponent hits the mat, start your backward step and when he is
clear of you, leap away from him.

375

376

377

RISING FROM THE MAT

If you have been thrown and your opponent player is standing
near you, you must rise correctly or you will be vulnerable
to a second throw or mat work.

375, 376. Here the thrown player arises incorrectly. He is too
close to the other player and has maintained his right hand grip.
He is thus wide open for a throw as he moves into the weak
position midway between kneeling and standing.

377. The right way: Slide away from the opponent. Turn your
body so that your feet are toward him and rise at a safe distance
from him.

378

379

STANDING CHOKES & THROWS IN COMBINATION

Standing chokes can be used in combination with throwing techniques or as feinting tactics.

In combination, you may have tried to apply a choke, without success. As your opponent reacts to the choke, take advantage of his diverted attention to try a throw.

As a feint or faking tactic, simulate the choke attempt and throw when he responds to the feint.

378. A choke is attempted and the opponent player resists.

379. The throw is applied.

THE THIRTY-SECOND TEST

If you are matched with an opponent whom you have not observed in contest, use the first thirty seconds of the match to discover strengths and weaknesses, or idiosyncrasies which you might use to your advantage.

The following are drawing-out actions--feints. You will use the information you gain to set up point-winning tactics.

Feint an arm action as though attempting a body throw. Note the reaction.

Fake a leg throw attempt. Note the response.

Feint a left side throw attempt.

Feint a standing choke attempt.

Make a low cloth grab.

The response of the opponent player to any of these feints will reveal defense gestures and style and will give a good judo player clues to planning a winning strategy.

CHANGING STYLE AS A TACTIC

In high level judo tournament, contestants can "read" an opponent's style after watching a match, or within the first half-minute of contest with him. An experienced player can use that information for defense and in planning an offense strategy.

Conversely, as you gain experience and skill, you can avoid exposing your style by using tactics which might mislead the opponent player.

COUNTERTHROWS

The kinds and numbers of combinations of tactical moves in judo are, for all practical purposes, limitless. The more you play, the more flexible you will become in combining techniques and tactics. Every session of judo randori is a fresh game of actions, responses, and counteractions.

Here is an example of the tactical use of counterthrowing.

380. The left player attempts a sweeping-foot throw . . .

381. . . . which the right player evades by going with the movement, allowing his foot to be swept as he turns counterclockwise, and finishes in a body throw position.

380

381

DIGEST OF JUDO CONTEST RULES

Before entering a contest, each player should have the specific
contest rules, in writing, well in advance of the date of the
contest. There are variations in contest rules and players
should know how qualifying matches are conducted, which
techniques might be prohibited, the duration of matches, the
point-scoring system, and all other details of the tournament
rules and regulations.

The following summary covers the general rules of international judo tournament.

Judo is played on a mat 9 meters (approximately 30 feet)
square, which is surrounded by a safety area of not less than
2½ meters.

Matches are from 3 to 20 minutes long, with extensions of
from 2 to 7 minutes. The duration of the matches and of the
extensions are arranged in advance.

One referee and four judges officiate. Sometimes there will
be a referee and two judges, and there are contests for which
there is only a referee. Records and time are kept by officials
on the side line.

Contestants are matched according to weight classes. Some
old-style judo clubs continue to match contestants by belt
rank, regardless of size and weight.

The regulation judo uniform must be worn, with a red or
white ribbon tied over the belt. The judges use a red flag
and a white flag to indicate scoring by the "red" or "white"
player.

Contestants are required to be clean and to wear a clean
uniform. Their fingernails and toenails must be short and
smooth. It is prohibited to wear any ornaments or articles
which might hurt the opponent player.

Contestants stand facing each other about 4 meters (about
12 feet) apart. They make a standing bow. The contest
begins with the announcement of *hajime* by the referee.
Contestants must be standing at the start of the contest.

Points are scored for throwing techniques and for grappling
techniques. The match is ended when one of the contestants
scores a full point (*ippon*).

A point-scoring throw must put the opponent on his back or side and the thrower must not lose his balance. Half-points (*waza ari*) may be awarded for throws completed with almost acceptable techniques.

Quarter-points and eighth-points are awarded for style and for incomplete attempts. They are also given to the player whose opponent plays excessively in the defense mode or as penalty points for minor infractions.

Matwork may be applied after an opponent has been thrown or if the opponent puts himself on the mat (by falling or by attempting a sacrificing throw) but the opponent may not be dragged or wrestled down onto the mat for the purpose of applying a grappling technique.

Unlike wrestling, which requires that the opponent be pinned to the mat, grappling in judo may be applied with the opponent standing (chokes), prone, or supine. If the opponent cannot escape from the hold, or if he submits within 30 seconds, a point may be scored.

Among the hand signals are:

> Full point scored (*ippon*)--one hand raised high above the head.

> Half-point scored (*waza ari*)--one hand extended, shoulder-high, palm down.

> Invalid technique--one hand raised and waved.

> Time (*jikan*)--one hand extended, shoulder-high, palm toward the timekeeper.

To stop the contest, the referee calls *sono mama*; to resume play, he calls *yoshi*.

If the time expires before a full point is scored, the referee announces "that is all" (*sore made*) to end the match. Judges and/or referees may award a win by decision on the basis of superior technique or by default.

To end the contest, the referee announces *sore made*.

The contestants return to the starting position and bow to each other after the result of the contest has been announced.

ILLEGAL CONTEST TACTICS

In judo contest, it is illegal to use any tactic which causes pain or might injure the opponent player. There are judo contests in which some holds and chokes are legal and others are not. Some throws are not permitted in some contests. The written rules of the contest should specify prohibited techniques.

Among illegal tactics are:

Attempting to throw an opponent by intertwining a leg around his leg.

Applying leg scissors.

Applying any joint lock except to the elbow.

Applying any technique which might injure the neck or spine.

Deliberately hurting the opponent in order to make him vulnerable to a throwing attempt.

Intentionally falling backwards onto the opponent.

An excessively defensive stance or excessively defensive mode of play.

Hand and foot blows are not permitted in judo contest, nor are poking, shoving, elbowing or knuckling tactics.

Sometimes rough or illegal tactics are used which are not clearly visible to the judges. Some examples are:

382. From a standard grip, the knuckle of the right hand is digging into the chest, causing pain.

383. Pivoting in for a throw, the right elbow is rammed into the solar plexus, causing extreme pain.

384. Instead of using a standard sweep, the side of the foot is used to strike a painful blow into the shin.

385. In the pivot, the knee strikes the player's thigh to hurt and weaken him.

If an illegal tactic seems to be accidental you might overlook it. But when illegal actions seem deliberate and occur repeatedly or when the opponent player is so clumsy or rough that there is a risk of injury, you should decline to finish the match.

The procedure for declining play is: Back away from your opponent and bow. Explain to the officials the reason why you are declining to finish.

382

383

384

385

386

BLACK BELT FORMAL THROWS—SHODAN NAGA NO KATA

This is a long routine of fifteen throws in five sets of three throws each. The candidate for promotion to black belt is expected to perform the routine with a high degree of technical excellence.

The gestures in the kata combine sport-like beginning positions with old-style "self-defense" reminiscent of ancient jujitsu forms. A modern alternative to the "self-defense" movements in the katas are given in parentheses. In my view, the modified form is more appropriate for present-day practice of judo. I have adapted the old-style jujitsu self-defense katas in another book.*

In the old style, the candidates walk onto the mat and face each other at a distance of about three and a half meters (approximately twelve feet); they turn to face the judges. In unison they bow to the judge; then they turn to face each other.

386. Lowering themselves in a slow and graceful manner, they kneel with the right knee on the mat and . . .

387. . . . after a brief hesitation, they place the left knee on the mat.

388. They sit on their heels and place their hands at their thighs.

389. Placing their hands onto the mat, they bow in unison.

---

*Bruce Tegner's Complete Book of Jujitsu, Thor, 1977

387

388

389

Then, in reverse order, they repeat the movements, rising to the standing position. In unison, they take sliding steps, advancing the left foot first, until they are about one meter (approximately three feet) apart. They hesitate briefly, then each takes a small step with the left foot to within arms' reach, ready to demonstrate the throws.

In the modern style, candidates for promotion walk onto the mat in a slow, dignified manner; they bow to the instructor and/ or judges; they bow to each other and then grasp in the standard throwing position and begin the demonstration.

Candidates will have practiced the forms for months before making this demonstration. Their timing and their coordinated movements should be perfect and beautiful. There is no competition involved in the demonstration and both partners cooperate fully. There is complete concentration on technical proficiency.

The fifteen throws of the black belt kata are:

a. Pulling-down throw--Uki otoshi
b. Shoulder throw--Seoi nage
c. Shouldering throw--Kata guruma
d. Hip throw--Uki goshi
e. Sweeping-thigh throw--Hari goshi
f. Levering-arm hip throw--Tsurikomi goshi
g. Side sweeping-foot throw--Okuri ashi harai
h. Lifting sweeping-foot throw--Sasae tsurikomi ashi
i. Upper innercut throw--Uchi mata
j. Circle throw--Tomoe nage
k. Back body sacrifice throw--Ura nage
l. Inside lateral sacrifice throw--Sumi gaeshi
m. Rear sweeping-foot/takedown throw--Yoko gake
n. Side body sacrifice throw--Yoko guruma
o. Ankle lateral sacrifice throw--Uki waza

390. From the standard starting position, tori, in the grey uniform, takes a step forward with his right foot as uke takes a step back with his left foot.

391. Uke steps forward with his right foot as tori lowers himself onto his left knee.

Using a wheeling arm movement, tori throws . . .

392. . . . and uki falls on his left side. At this level of proficiency, uke will be able to spring up and take a crisp, high-arc fall even though the throwing action is from a standstill.

They hesitate briefly. Uke rises to a kneeling position. In unison, both rise to the standing position. The throw is demonstrated on the other side.

390

391

392

393

394

395

393. The next throw, in the old style, begins with an exaggerated gesture of hitting. Tori blocks with his forearm. (Modern style: uke reaches forward as though to grip tori for a throwing action.)

394. Tori responds by pivoting, dropping his right arm . . .

395. . . . and moving into position for the arm-around-shoulder hip throw. Tori completes the throw, steps into a "T" stance to demonstrate good ending balance, then he takes a natural stance and waits until uke rises and faces him, ready to demonstrate the same throw on the right side.

They return to the starting position. In unison, tori and uke grip cloth.

396

397

396. Tori takes a step forward with his right foot as uke steps back on his left foot, in position for tori to . . .

397. . . . apply the shouldering throw.

The throw is repeated on the other side. They return to the starting position.

398

399

398. Uke makes a threatening gesture, as though to hit tori with the side of his fist. (Modern style: uke reaches forward as though to grasp cloth.)

399. Tori sidesteps and pivots clockwise, in position to apply a hip throw on the left side. He throws, takes a "T" stance and then a natural stance while uke rises to face him.

They repeat the hip throw on the right side. They return to the starting position. From a standstill, they grip cloth in unison.

400

401

402

400. Tori pivots counterclockwise . . .

401. . . . and executes a sweeping-thigh throw, which uke assists by springing up as the throw is applied.

They repeat the throw on the other side. They return to the starting position. From a standstill, they grip cloth in unison.

402. Tori pivots into position for an arm-around-the-neck throw. Uke pulls back and crouches slightly.

403   404

403. Tori then shifts his weight so that he is in a very low, hip-throwing position. Keeping his right arm rigidly extended, he grips cloth at uke's back collar . . .

404. . . . and he applies a hip throw with a levering arm action.

405   406

They repeat the throw on the other side and return to the starting position.

405. They grasp cloth and take two gliding, circular steps in unison.

406. As uke takes another gliding step, tori puts his left foot in position to apply a side sweeping-foot throw . . .

407

407. . . . which he times so that both of uke's feet are swept up.

408

409

The throw is repeated on the other side. They return to the starting position.

They grasp cloth, and . . .

408. . . . tori pulls uke forward as he places his foot on uke's right instep and . . .

409. . . . applies a lifting sweeping-foot throw, which uke assists by springing up as the throw is executed.

They repeat the throw on the other side and return to the starting position.

410   411

410. In unison, they take two big gliding, circular steps to reverse their positions . . .

411. . . . so that uke is now on the left.

412   413

412. As uke takes another gliding step, tori applies . . .

413. . . . the upper innercut throw.

They repeat the throw on the other side and then return to the starting position.

414

415

416

414. As tori takes a step forward on his right foot, uke takes a step backward on his left foot.

415. Tori places his foot at uke's belt as uke shifts his weight forward . . .

416. . . . and assists the circle throw by rolling over and out.

They repeat the throw, tori placing his left foot at uke's belt and uke taking the fall with his right arm advanced. They return to the starting position.

417

418

417. Uke makes a threatening gesture, as though to hit tori with the side of his fist. (Modern style: uke reaches forward as though to grip cloth for a throw.)

418. Uke takes a deep step forward as tori sidesteps around to uke's right side and puts his hands at uke's back and stomach . . .

419

420

419. . . . pulling uke's body in close to him; tori leans back and twists his body counterclockwise and . . .

420. . . . applies a back body sacrifice throw by falling directly upon his back as he twists uke around to fall at his left side.

The throw is repeated on the other side and they return to the starting position.

421

422

421. From the starting position, they take a step in unison and lock their heads at each other's right shoulder, as shown. (Modern style: eliminate the "wrestling" gesture.)

422. Uke shifts his weight forward as tori pulls back, lowers himself to the mat and executes a right-side inside lateral sacrifice throw.

The throw is repeated on the left side and they return to the starting position.

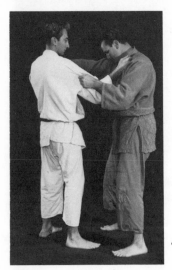

423

424

423. Tori twists uke counterclockwise as he steps to uke's right side . . .

424. . . . and applies a rear sweeping-foot sacrifice throw . . .

425

425. . . . carrying the swept foot high and falling back with uke so that both are on the mat at the completion of the throw.

The throw is repeated on the left side and they return to the starting position.

426

427

Uke threatens tori with a fist blow gesture. (Modern style: uke reaches as though to grip cloth and throw.)

426. As uke's arm comes forward, tori sidesteps to place himself at uke's right side and puts his hands at uke's back and stomach.

427. Tori slides his right foot between uke's feet as he twists uke counterclockwise with arm and body movement . . .

428

429

430

431

428. . . . to apply a side body sacrifice throw. Tori falls on his back as he wheels uke around and over; uke falls at tori's side.

They repeat the throw on the other side and then return to the starting position.

429. They simulate a stylized wrestling posture. (Modern style: the throw is applied from a standstill.)

430. Placing his left foot at uke's right ankle . . .

431. . . . tori applies an ankle lateral sacrifice throw.

The throw is repeated on the other side and then they return to the starting position.

Taking steps in unison, they back away from each other until they are about three and a half meters (approximately twelve feet) apart. Then they repeat the opening salutation, in reverse order. They walk off the mat in a slow, formal manner.

This completes the routine.

PROCEDURE

Both men walk onto the mat with slow, dignified steps and stand facing each other about three and a half meters (approximately twelve feet) apart. In unison, they turn and bow to the instructor, then bow to each other. They kneel and then rise onto the left knee with the right foot on the mat. Uke pivots on his left knee and lies supine on the mat. Tori either rises and walks toward uke and kneels at his side, or without rising, tori slides toward uke and kneels at his side . . .

432. . . . as shown. Uke is passive throughout the form. He allows tori to apply the mat work without resistance. This is a formal demonstration of technique.

432

HOLDS — OSEA WAZA

SIDE SHOULDER HOLD

433. With slow, deliberate movements, tori places uke's right arm under his (tori's) left arm.

433

434

434. Then he reaches around uke's neck with his right hand and takes a side shoulder hold. He hesitates briefly and then returns to the kneeling position at uke's side.

435

436

437

SIDE SHOULDER HOLD WITH ARM LOCK

435. From the kneeling position tori . . .

436. . . . pushes uke's right arm across uke's face . . .

437. . . . and applies the side shoulder hold with an arm lock.
He hesitates briefly and then returns to the kneeling position.

438

439

440

TOP-BODY HOLD

438. From the kneeling position, tori rises and walks around behind uke's head and kneels.

439. He slides both his hands under uke's shoulders . . .

440. . . . and grips uke's belt, locks his elbows firmly into uke's sides and takes a top-body hold. He hesitates briefly and then returns to the kneeling position.

441

442

CROSS-BODY HOLD WITH HEAD-AND-LEG LOCK

441. From the kneeling position, tori reaches under uke's bent left leg . . .

442. . . . and grips uke's belt with his right hand. With his left hand he reaches around to grip uke's collar. He hesitates briefly, then returns to the kneeling position.

443

TOP-BODY HOLD WITH ARM LOCK

From the kneeling position, tori rises and walks around and kneels behind uke's head.

443. With his right hand, tori raises uke's right arm and locks it under his right armpit with his elbow. He grips cloth at uke's right side with his right hand.

444

444. He applies the top-body hold and hesitates briefly. He rises and returns to the kneeling position at uke's side.

He hesitates again, briefly, then slides away from his partner, about half a meter (approximately eighteen inches), hesitates again and then, in unison, partners rise and walk to face each other about three and a half meters (approximately twelve feet) apart. Both kneel onto the left knee. Both men now retie their belts and straighten their jackets, ready for the next set, the chokes.

CHOKES—SHIME WAZA

NO PRESSURE IS APPLIED in the demonstration of the choke holds. Evaluation of technique is made on the basis of simulated holds. The instructor should caution tori to avoid any pressure and should caution uke to tap for release if pressure is applied.

CROSS-ARM CHOKE

Uke returns to the supine position. Tori kneels at his side.

445. With his left hand, tori grips uke's left collar with his thumb outside the jacket.

445

446

447

446. As he straddles uke's body, tori grips uke's right collar with his right hand.

447. He simulates a cross-arm choke as he places his head down on the mat next to uke's head. He holds the position briefly and then returns to the kneeling position.

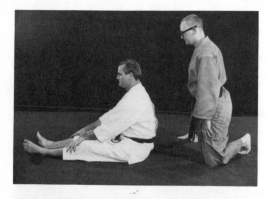

448

REAR ONE-ARM CHOKE

448. From the kneeling position, tori rises and walks around to kneel about one meter (approximately three feet) behind uke's head as uke rises to a seated position.

449

450

451

449. On his knees, tori slides up close to uke and . . .

450. . . . puts his right arm around uke's neck . . .

451. . . . and grips his own right wrist with his left hand, placing his head onto uke's left shoulder.

The choke is *simulated* without pressure. Tori hesitates briefly, then returns to kneel behind uke.

452

REAR LAPEL CHOKE

452. With his left hand, tori reaches under uke's left arm and grips cloth at the right lapel . . .

453

454

453. . . . and with his right hand reaches over to grip cloth at uke's left shoulder.

454. The choke is simulated as tori pulls cloth back with both hands as tori braces his head into uke's shoulder. Even in simulation, tori does not apply pressure to the front of uke's throat. Tori hesitates briefly, then returns to the kneeling position behind uke.

455

CHOKE WITH HALF NELSON

455. Tori slides his left hand under uke's left arm . . .

456

456. . . . and places his left hand behind uke's head. With his right hand, tori reaches around uke's neck to grip cloth at uke's left collar. The choke is simulated by straightening both arms. Tori hesitates briefly, then rises. Uke lies down and tori kneels at his side.

457

458

CROSS-ARM CHOKE WITH FOOT LEVERAGE

457. With his left hand, tori grips cloth at uke's left collar . . .

458. . . . and straddles uke as he grips cloth at uke's right collar with the right hand.

459

460

459. The choke is simulated; tori rolls toward uke's side as he simulates the choking action.

460. Uke follows the rolling action, rolling with tori's movement. Now tori is on his back and adds foot leverage to the simulated choking pressure, placing both his feet at uke's belt.

After a brief hesitation, both men return to the kneeling position, facing each other. They retie their belts and straighten their uniforms and are ready for the next set, the locks.

LOCKS—KENSETSU WAZA

The locks are applied with *very light pressure.* Uke should not feel pain; if he does, he should tap for release and tori should be cautioned.

BENT-ARM LOCK

461. Uke lies down. Tori kneels at his side. Uke raises his arm.

461

462

462. With his left hand tori grips uke's raised wrist and bends
it toward uke's shoulder. With his right hand, tori reaches under
the captured arm . . .

463

463. . . . to grip his own left wrist as he leans across uke's upper
body. Applying light pressure, tori demonstrates the technique
by pulling both arms toward himself. He hesitates briefly and
then returns to the kneeling position at uke's side.

464

STRAIGHT-ARM LOCK WITH HIP PRESSURE

464. Uke raises his right arm.

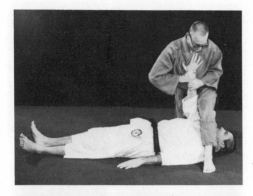

465

466

465. Tori grips the raised wrist with both hands, and places his left leg across uke's neck.

466. Tori lies back onto the mat and wedges his right foot into uke's side and draws the captured arm across his thigh. Tori simulates the lock (with very light pressure) by raising his hips. He hesitates briefly, then returns to the kneeling position at uke's side.

467

STRAIGHT-ARM LOCK WITH SHOULDER PRESSURE

467. Uke raises his left arm. Tori is ready to grip the raised arm with both hands.

468

468. He captures the upper arm and pulls uke's straight arm into his chest as he levers forward with his shoulder. After a brief hesitation, he returns to the kneeling position at uke's side.

STRAIGHT-ARM LOCK WITH LEG PRESSURE

Both partners rise to a standing position and grasp in the standard manner for throwing.

469. In unison they kneel with their left knees on the mat.

469

470

470. Tori makes a gesture as though to hit uke with an open hand; uke releases his right hand grip.

471. Then tori captures uke's right arm under his left arm and locks it into his side; tori puts his right foot at uke's left knee.

471

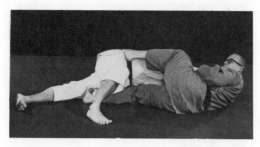

472

472. Tori rolls onto his right side and pushes uke's knee with his right foot. As he rolls, tori crosses his left leg over the captured arm. Pressure is applied lightly by levering down with the left leg and pushing with the right foot. After a brief hesitation, they return to a kneeling position facing each other.

SITTING DOWN TWO-ARM LOCK

473. From the kneeling position, they rise in unison and grasp in the standard throwing position.

474. Tori lowers himself onto the mat, sliding between uke's feet . . .

475. . . . gripping cloth at uke's elbows and pressing in to lock uke's arms. Tori curls his left around uke's right leg . . .

476. . . . and tori topples uke over toward his (tori's) right side, twisting uke's arms by maintaining his hand grips.

477. Tori applies light pressure by pressing his left leg into uke's body, locking uke's leg and forcing uke's head and shoulder onto the mat. Uke's arms are straight and locked.

The position is held briefly, then both partners rise to the kneeling position, facing each other. Then they repeat the salutation in reverse order, before leaving the mat with slow, formal steps.

This completes the routine.

473

474

475

476

477

COUNTERTHROWING FORMS—GONOSEN NO KATA

This set of formal counterthrowing moves is a prearranged, rehearsed series in which uke, demonstrated by Robert Simmons, simulates an attempted throw, to which tori, demonstrated by Elise Simmons, responds with a counter-throw. In the demonstration, the throw is carried through, tori ends in a well-balanced "T" stance and uke hesitates briefly after being thrown, then rises to face tori in the starting position.

The countering moves in this set are:

Uke:	Tori counters with:
a. Kickback throw	Kickback throw
Osoto gari	Osoto gari
b. Kneeblock wheeling throw	Kneeblock wheeling throw
Hiza guruma	Hiza guruma
c. Innercut throw	Back sweeping-foot throw
O uchi gari	Ko soto gari
d. Front sweeping-foot throw	Front sweeping-foot throw
De ashi harai	De ashi harai
e. Outercut throw	Straight-leg throw
Ko soto kake	Tai otoshi
f. Inside sweeping-foot throw	Lifting sweeping-foot throw
Ko uchi gari	Harai tsurikomi ashi
g. Arm-around-neck hip throw	Rear hip throw
Kochi guruma	Ushiro goshi
h. Hip throw	Left side hip throw
Tsurikomi goshi	Uki goshi
j. Sweeping-thigh throw	Rear hip throw
Harai goshi	Ushiro goshi
k. Upper innercut	Rear hip throw
Uchi mata	Ushiro goshi
l. Shoulder throw	Inside lateral sacrifice
Seoi nage	Sumi gaeshi

486   487

486. From the starting position, he simulates an attempted outercut throw . . .

487. . . . and she counters with a straight-leg throw.

488   489

488. From the starting position, he simulates an attempted inside sweeping-foot throw . . .

489. . . . which she counters with a lifting sweeping-foot throw.

490   491

490. From the starting position, he simulates an attempted arm-around-neck hip throw . . .

491. . . . which she counters with a rear hip throw.

492   493

492. From the starting position, he simulates an attempted hip throw . . .

493. . . . she counters with a left side throw.

494   495

494. From the starting position, he simulates a spring-leg throw . . .

495. . . . and she counters with a lifting sweeping-foot throw.

496   497

496. From the starting position, he simulates an attempted sweeping-thigh throw . . .

497. . . . which she counters, using a rear hip throw.

498   499

498. He simulates an upper innercut throwing attempt . . .

499. . . . which she counters, using a rear hip throw.

500   501

500. From the starting position, he simulates an attempted shoulder throw . . .

501. . . . which she counters, using an inside lateral sacrifice throw.

They both hesitate briefly before rising and returning to the starting position. They repeat the salutation bowing, in reverse order, before leaving the mat.

This completes the routine.

INDEX

FOR A FREE DESCRIPTIVE BROCHURE
describing our complete line of BRUCE TEGNER
books on karate, judo, self-defense, kung fu,
tai chi and other specialty titles in this field,
as well as ELLEN KEI HUA'S inspirational
books, write to:

THOR PUB. CO.
P. O. BOX 1782
VENTURA CA 93002